ACKNOWLEDGMENTS

We wish to express our heartfelt gratitude to the following people who have helped make this book possible:

First and foremost, we would like to thank our families for their patience, love, and support throughout this process.

Patty Aubery for her vision, commitment, and humor. Tina Renga for her joy and boundless enthusiasm; Russ Kamalski and Roger Conner for their guidance, faith, and stamina throughout this project. All of you have been there for us every step of the way on this journey, and you have filled it with wisdom, love, and laughter.

Our book publisher and friend, Peter Vegso, for his continued support on this new venture, as well as the entire staff at Health Communications, Inc.

Veronica Romero, Lisa Williams, Robin Yerian, Jesse Ianniello, Lauren Edelstein, and Lauren Bray, who support Jack's businesses with skill and love.

We are truly grateful and love you all!

Jack Canfield and D.D. Watkins

In Gratitude

D.D. would like to express a special thank you to her daughter Marissa for her patience throughout this project and for being a constant source of beauty and inspiration, her stepson Christian for inherently knowing how to believe and receive, and Lee for loving me enough to set me free when I needed to fly. I am grateful every single day for the support and encouragement of my sisters, Melanie, Stephanie, and Polly, and for the creativity, grace, and gentility of my mother, Martha, who taught me long ago to love words, poetry, and all things beautiful. Vicki, Randi, Georgia, Gram, Daddy, and Frank—my teachers and companions on this journey . . . I love you all, I always will, and I am grateful.

INTRODUCTION

It is said that when the student is ready, the teacher will appear. If you are reading this book, then you are obviously ready to take the next step in your own personal evolution. You are ready to begin deliberately creating and receiving more of what you really want in your life. By consciously and intentionally working with the Law of Attraction, you can create exactly what you want with less effort and more joy.

While many people now refer to the Law of Attraction as a "secret," it is neither a new concept nor a recent discovery. It has been an integral part of the great teachings of the ages for several millennia. I have been teaching this principle, along with many others, for over thirty years. With the release of the DVD movie *The Secret* and appearances by many of the teachers (myself included) that were featured in the movie on *Oprah, Larry King Live, The Today Show, Montel, The Ellen Degeneres Show,* and *Nightline,* the awareness of the Law of Attraction has now become part of the mainstream culture.

Finally, we are learning that we are all participants in the creation of our lives, and we are all responsible for the state of the world we live in. We are beginning to realize that if we want things to change on an external level, then we must be willing to make the necessary internal changes as well. There is a shift taking place, a change in our awareness. This change is in the air and on the airwaves, and we can feel it deep within our souls. There seems to be a common yearning among us to return to a simpler, more joyous place and time, and we know on some internal level that there is more to life than what we have been experiencing. We know that greater fulfillment is possible and we are ready for it. We have reached a point where we have come full circle in our spiritual evolution, and we are longing to understand our connection to each other, our purpose, and ourselves. We are, as a people, looking within, questioning our priorities, our circumstances, and searching for deeper meaning in our lives.

It is my hope that through this book and through a better understanding of how the Law of Attraction is at work in your life, you will also gain a greater understanding of yourself—a sense of who you really are and why you are here. This simple guide is your key. It can unlock the gate to the future you desire and lead you down a path of greater joy, prosperity, and abundance. It is my intention that as you read this book you will find yourself inspired by the realization that you *can* create the life you desire, and that you will be empowered by the use of the basic tools, strategies, and concepts contained within these pages.

This book is in your hands for a reason. You can begin to live a truly conscious life—one that is filled with purpose and meaning—right now. Starting today, you can begin to reconnect with your inner truth and wisdom. You can learn to trust your intuition, heighten your awareness, and honor your emotions. By simply trusting in the natural order of things, and by trusting in a higher power than yourself, you can learn to let go and begin living in a place of real faith, gratitude, and joy. As you make these changes, you will start to become increasingly aware of the miracles all around you; and the events in your life will begin to unfold in what seem like magical and mysterious ways.

Remember, you are inextricably connected to everyone and everything in the universe, including God. You always have been. At any given moment the universe is automatically responding to your every thought, feeling, and action. It has no choice; it's simply the way things work. It acts as a mirror, reflecting back to you the very energy you project. The thoughts and energy that you send out into the universe will always attract back to you, in one form or another, things and experiences that match those thoughts and energy. This is the Law of Attraction at work in your life. It is a perfect example of this brilliantly designed universe in action, an immutable universal law. The Law of Attraction is the scientific explanation for coincidence, serendipity, and the power of prayer.

Knowing this, if you want to find greater happiness and fulfillment in your life, you must begin to live in harmony with the natural rhythm of the universe, and in harmony with the Law of Attraction. You must choose to live in a place of gratitude, greater peace, and higher consciousness. You must learn to follow your bliss, do what you love, and make time to find joy in your life. It is your natural birthright to be happy, and it is your obligation to express yourself through your natural gifts and talents in a way that brings you joy. By doing so, you are also making an essential contribution to the world we live in.

Imagine a world where we are all living in this way. A world where we all take full responsibility for our thoughts, our actions, and the results they produce, and become more loving, giving, compassionate, and appreciative people. Through the Law of Attraction the natural result of all of these things is a state of ever increasing joy and abundance. As we become happier, more grateful individuals, we create a vibrational match for all the good that the universe has to offer, and we begin to shift the energy of the entire planet.

This is the key to authentic success.
This is the key to Living the Law of Attraction.

Your journey begins right here, right now. Empower yourself—use this key, unlock the gate, and take this simple path I am offering you.

I will guide you each step of the way. Living the Law of Attraction in a conscious, deliberate way will change your life, and it will change the way you participate in this global community. You can change the way you think, you can change your life, and you can change the world. Start living the life you are meant to live. You are here for a reason, and the world needs what you have to offer.

Envision the future you desire.
Create the life of your dreams.

See it, feel it, believe it.

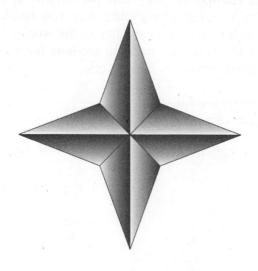

*To trust in the force
that moves the universe is faith.
Faith isn't blind, it's visionary.
Faith is believing that the universe
is on our side, and that the universe
knows what it's doing.*

Author Unknown

(1)
LAW OF ATTRACTION

Understanding the Law of Attraction is the key to creating the life of your dreams.

The Law of Attraction is the most powerful law in the universe. Just like gravity, it is always in effect, always in motion. *It is working in your life at this very moment.*

Simply put, the Law of Attraction says that you will attract into your life whatever you focus on. Whatever you give your energy and attention to will come back to you. So, if you stay focused on the good and positive things in your life, you will automatically attract more good and positive things into your life. If you are focused upon lack and negativity, then *that* is what will be attracted into your life.

> ***You are what you think about***
> ***all day long.***
> *Dr. Robert Schuller*

You are *always* in a state of creation. You always have been. You are creating your reality in every moment of every day. You are creating your future with every single thought: either consciously or subconsciously. You can't take a break from it and decide *not* to create because creation never stops. The Law of Attraction never stops working.

So, understanding just how this law operates is a fundamental key to your success. If you want to change your life, and empower yourself to create an amazing future, then you need to understand your role in the Law of Attraction.

> **To let life happen to you is irresponsible.**
> **To create your day is your divine right.**
> *Ramtha*

Here's how it works: Like attracts like. If you are feeling excited, enthusiastic, passionate, happy, joyful, appreciative, or abundant, then you are sending out *positive* energy. On the other hand, if you are feeling bored, anxious, stressed out, angry, resentful, or sad, you are sending out *negative* energy. The universe, through the Law of Attraction, will respond enthusiastically to both of these vibrations. It doesn't decide which one is better for you, it just responds to *whatever* energy you are creating, and it gives you more of the same. You get back exactly what you put out there. Whatever you are thinking and feeling at any given time is basically your request to the universe for more of the same.

Because your energy vibrations will attract energy back to you of the same frequencies, you need to make sure that you are continually sending out energy, thoughts, and feelings that resonate with what you want to be, do, and experience. Your energy frequencies need to be in tune with what you want to attract in your life. If love and joy are what you want to attract, then the vibrational frequencies of love and joy are what you want to create.

Think of it this way—it's a lot like transmitting and receiving radio waves. Your frequency has to match the frequency of what you want to receive. You can't tune your radio to 98.7 on your FM dial and expect to get a station broadcasting on 103.3. It just won't happen. Your energy has to synchronize with, or match, the energy frequency of the sender. So, you have to keep your vibration tuned to a positive frequency in order to attract positive energy back to you.

Another good example is that of a tuning fork. When you strike a tuning fork you activate it to send out a particular sound or frequency. Now, in a room filled with tuning forks—*only* those that are tuned to the exact same frequency will begin to vibrate in response. They will automatically connect and respond to the frequency that matches their own. So the idea here is to tune *yourself* to resonate at a frequency that is in harmony with what you want to attract. In order to create a positive future, you need to keep your energy, thoughts, and feelings in the positive range.

You can learn to manage your thoughts and emotions and maintain a vibrational match for what you want to attract by learning to respond instead of just reacting to the situations in your life. Most of us go through life just reacting automatically and unconsciously to the things and events that take place around us. Perhaps you're having a rough day, you've gotten a flat tire, or maybe someone has treated you unfairly. Say that you react in a negative way to these situations with your thoughts and your emotions. You become angry, frustrated, or upset. In this case, you are unconsciously *reacting* to the situation instead of consciously *responding* to it, and your negatively charged thoughts and emotions are automatically placing an order with the universe for more of the same negative experiences. In order to create a more positive outcome, you must learn to consciously respond in a different, more positive way.

> *If you do what you've always done, you'll get what you've always gotten.*
> Anthony Robbins

The good news is that once you understand the Law of Attraction, and how it works, you can begin to consciously and intentionally create a better life. You can *choose* to respond differently to the situations that arise during your day. You can *choose* to think differently. You can *choose* to focus and think about the things you want more of in your life. You can *choose* to experience more of the things that make you feel good. You can *choose* to deliberately participate in the creation of your future by managing your thoughts and feelings.

> *Your future is created by what you do*
> *today, not tomorrow.*
> Robert Kiyosaki

Expect miracles.

The Law of Attraction allows for *infinite* possibilities, *infinite* abundance, and *infinite* joy. It knows no order of difficulty, and it can change your life in every way.

In order to really understand how the Law of Attraction works in your life, we need to look at a few things.

Let's start at the beginning.

> *The universe is change; our life*
> *is what our thoughts make it.*
> Marcus Aurelius Antoninus

(2)
WHAT YOU ARE

You are energy.

Pure and simple. You are made up of the same stuff as the sun, the moon, and the stars. You are a walking, talking bundle of intelligent energy in the form of a human body. You are made up of cells, which are made up of atoms, which are made up of subatomic particles. What are subatomic particles? ENERGY!

Everything is energy.

All matter is energy.

Energy cannot be created or destroyed.

It is the cause and effect of itself.

It is evenly present in all places, at all times.

Energy is in constant motion and never rests.

It is forever moving from one form to another.

ENERGY FOLLOWS THOUGHT.

There are no extra pieces in the universe.
Everyone is here because he or she
has a place to fill, and every piece must fit
itself into the big jigsaw puzzle.

Deepak Chopra

You are connected.

You are connected to everything and everyone. You are a completely unique piece of a much greater whole, an integral part of the cosmos. You are a ball of energy in a much larger energy field. You are part of a much greater power; you are part of God. The wisdom of the entire universe is yours for the asking.

Think of the Internet. You can't see it or touch it but you know that it is there. It is real. It is an invisible energy connection that links us all to each other. You are connected to everyone and everything in much the same way.

Have you ever found that with people you are close to, you can sometimes finish a sentence for them, or that you both say the same thing at exactly the same time? This is not coincidence, it's connection! This is a perfect example of how connected we really are to those around us.

We've all had the experience of starting to think about someone, perhaps someone we haven't even seen or spoken to in years, and then several minutes later the phone rings, and it is them on the other end of the line. "I was just thinking about you," we exclaim in wonder. We were actually picking up on their *intention* to call us before they had even acted upon it. Our thoughts travel through time and space at an amazing speed. Through your connection you were able to pick up on the energy of their thoughts and intentions before they even dialed the number, or perhaps it was your thinking about them that stimulated them to call you.

You are a magnet.

You are a living magnet. You *literally* attract the things, people, ideas, and circumstances to you that vibrate and resonate at the same energy frequency as yours. Your energy field changes constantly, based on your thoughts and feelings, and the universe acts like a mirror, sending back a reflection of the energy that you are projecting. The stronger and more intense your thoughts and emotions are, the greater the magnetic pull becomes. Now, this is not a process that requires any real effort; a magnet doesn't "try" to attract anything—it simply does, and so do you! You are always in the process of attracting *something* into your life.

Do you realize that your life at this very moment is the result of everything that you have ever thought, done, believed, or felt up until now? You can start right now to consciously and deliberately attract *whatever* you desire in this lifetime. Through the Law of Attraction you can attract people, resources, money, ideas, strategies, and circumstances— literally everything you need to create the future of your dreams.

All that we are is the result
of what we have thought.

Buddha

You are powerful.

You are far more powerful than you realize. You are creating everything in your life. Once you fully acknowledge this, and take responsibility for it, you can do *anything* that you set your mind to. You are the author of your own life, and you can choose to take it in any direction you wish.

You have the ability to change your life.
You have the ability to create your desired future.
You have *unlimited* potential!

> *Once you make a decision,*
> *the universe conspires*
> *to make it happen.*
>
> Ralph Waldo Emerson

(3)
WHO YOU ARE

Thoughts are things.

Your thoughts are not just wispy little clouds drifting through your head. Your thoughts are *things*. They are actually *measurable units of energy*. Thoughts are biochemical electrical impulses. They are waves of energy that, as far as we can tell, penetrate all time and space.

> *Thought is action in rehearsal.*
> *Sigmund Freud*

Your thoughts are powerful.
They are real, they are measurable, they are energy.

Every single thought you have is a statement of your desires to the universe. Every single thought you have generates a physiological change in your body. You are a product of all of the thoughts you have thought, feelings you have felt, and actions you have taken up until now. And ... the thoughts you think today, feelings you feel today, and actions you take today will determine your experiences tomorrow. So it is imperative that you learn to think and behave in a positive way that is in alignment with what you ultimately want to be, do, and experience in life.

The game of life is the game
of boomerangs. Our thoughts, deeds
and words return to us sooner or later,
with astounding accuracy.

Florence Shinn

Thoughts affect your body.

We know from polygraph, or lie detector tests, that your body
reacts to your thoughts. They change your temperature, heart
rate, blood pressure, breathing rate, muscle tension, and how
much your hands may sweat. Let's say you are hooked up to a
lie detector and asked a question like, "Did you take the
money?" If you *did* take the money and you lie about it, your
hands may sweat, or get colder, your heart will beat faster,
your blood pressure will go up, your breathing will get faster,
and your muscles will tighten. These kinds of physiological
reactions occur not only when you are lying, but in reaction to
every thought you have. *Every single cell in your body is
affected by every single thought you have!*

I admit thoughts influence the body.

Albert Einstein

So you can see the importance of learning to think as
positively as possible. Negative thoughts are toxic, and they
affect your body in a negative way. They weaken you, make
you perspire, create muscular tension, and even create a
more acidic environment within your body. They increase
the likelihood of cancer (cancer cells thrive in an acidic
environment) and other disease. They also send out a
negative energy vibration and attract more experiences of
the same vibration.

Positive thoughts, on the other hand, will affect your body in a positive way. They will make you feel more relaxed, more centered and alert. They stimulate the release of endorphins in your brain, reducing pain and increasing pleasure. In addition to this, your positive thoughts send out a positive energy vibration that will attract more positive experiences back into your life.

> *It has been proven now*
> *scientifically that an affirmative thought*
> *is hundreds of times more powerful*
> *than a negative thought.*
> Michael Bernard Beckwith

Your conscious and subconscious mind.

Most of us are fairly aware of our conscious thoughts, but it is important to become aware of our subconscious thoughts as well. Our subconscious mind is pretty much running the show, and since most of us have a constant negative tape playing in our heads, we are continually sending out negative messages. You must learn to reprogram your subconscious mind and transform your negative internal thoughts into healthy, positive ones. By looking closely at your beliefs and self-image, you can work on eliminating any limiting or negative ideas. This negative self-talk is like a type of static, or interference on a phone call. It will interfere with, distort, and even block the frequencies of your positive intentions. If not removed, it will reduce your ability to create and manifest the future you desire.

> *Sometimes you've got to let everything go . . .*
> *purge yourself. If you are unhappy*
> *with anything . . . whatever is bringing you down,*
> *get rid of it. Because you'll find that when you're free,*
> *your true creativity, your true self comes out.*
> Tina Turner

Unfortunately, many of us have a fairly stubborn tendency to hold on to our old negative thoughts and self-images. It's our comfort zone—we've become accustomed to our familiar concepts of reality, and we tend to get stuck in our subconscious beliefs of inadequacy, fear, and doubt. Most of these limiting thoughts and feelings stem from past incidents, beliefs, and experiences that we've internalized over the years and turned into our personal truths. These negative concepts can sabotage us and keep us from realizing our fullest growth and potential unless we make a conscious decision to address them, release them, and let them go.

Think about trying to drive a car with the parking brake on. No matter how much you try to accelerate, the parking brake will keep slowing you down, but as soon as you release it— you will automatically and effortlessly go faster. Your limiting thoughts, feelings, and behaviors are like a type of *psychological* parking brake. They will drag you down and slow you down unless you make a committed effort to let them go and replace them with more positive thoughts and beliefs.

You must be willing to release your negative mental programming and step out of your comfort zone in order to make room for a positive, healthy self-image and belief system. This will shift your energy vibration and allow you to more easily and effectively attract the positive energy and experiences that you desire in your life.

Beliefs are just your habitual thoughts, and they can be changed through affirmations, positive self-talk, behavioral changes, and visualization techniques. These are all extremely effective tools in releasing these old negative thought patterns, and we will address each of these powerful techniques in the chapters to come.

If you find that your negative programming is so deeply rooted that you are experiencing great difficulty in letting go, then you may want to try another approach. I have discovered three very powerful releasing techniques. They are extremely effective in the release of negative thought patterns, beliefs, and emotions. They are:

The Sedona Method by Hale Dwoskin
(www.sedonamethod.com)
The Work of Byron Katie
(www.TheWork.com)
The Emotional Freedom Technique
(www.emofree.com)

Each of these websites contains information on books, audio courses, and seminars that will help you learn how to quickly and powerfully release your negative mental programming and return to a place of pure awareness.

> **What the mind of man can
> conceive and believe, the mind
> of man can achieve.**
> *Napoleon Hill*

Your conscious mind.

The conscious mind is the part of you that thinks and reasons—it's the part of your mind that you use to make everyday decisions. Your free will lies here, and with your conscious mind, you can decide just what you want to create in your life. With this part of your mind you can accept or reject any idea. No person or circumstance can force you to think consciously about thoughts or ideas you do not choose. The thoughts you *do* choose, of course, will eventually deter-mine the course of your life. With practice, and a little bit of disciplined effort, you can learn to direct your thoughts to only those that will support the manifestation of your chosen dreams and goals. Your conscious mind is powerful, but it is the more limited part of your mind.

The conscious mind has:

Limited processing capacity

Short term memory (about 20 seconds)

The ability to manage 1 to 3 events at a time

Impulses that travel at 120 to 140 mph

The ability to process an average of 2,000
    bits of information per second

Your subconscious mind.

Your subconscious mind is actually much more spectacular. It is frequently referred to as your spiritual or universal mind, and it knows no limits except for those that *you* consciously choose. Your self-image and your habits live in your subconscious mind. It functions in every single cell of your body. This is the part of your mind that is connected to your Higher Self at a much greater level than your conscious mind. It is your connection to God, your connection to Source and Universal Infinite Intelligence.

Your subconscious mind is habitual and timeless, and it works in the present tense only. It stores your past learning experiences and memories, and it monitors all of your bodily operations, motor functions, heart rate, digestion, etc. Your subconscious mind thinks *literally*, and it will accept every thought that your conscious mind chooses to think. It has no ability to reject concepts or ideas. Now, what that means is that we can choose to use our conscious mind to deliberately reprogram our subconscious beliefs, and the subconscious mind *has* to accept the new ideas and beliefs; it can't reject them.

We can actually make a *conscious* decision to change the content of our *subconscious* mind!

The Subconscious Mind has:

Expanded processing capacity

Long term memory (past experiences,
   attitudes, values, and beliefs)

The ability to manage **thousands** of events
   at a time

Impulses that travel at over **100,000 mph**

The ability to process an average of
   4,000,000,000 bits of information
   per second

As you can see, the subconscious mind is *far* more powerful than the conscious mind. Think of your mind as an iceberg. The part of the iceberg you see, the part above water, is your *conscious* mind. It represents only about one sixth of your actual mental capacity, and the part below water (the other five sixths) is your subconscious mind. When we operate primarily from the conscious mind (as we typically do) we are only using a fraction of our true potential. The conscious mind is a much slower and more cumbersome vehicle than the subconscious mind.

So, the goal here is to learn to tap into the vast power of our subconscious mind in order to use it to our advantage. We must create room in each day to "check in" with our subconscious spiritual mind. Daily time spent quietly without any external distractions will strengthen our connection to who we really are. We can connect with our subconscious mind through the use of several techniques. They include: affirmations, visualization, prayer, contemplation and meditation, gratitude and appreciation, and the use of positive focus techniques.

Our subconscious mind can take us where we want to go and help us reach our goals in life much faster and more easily than our conscious mind ever could. So, by connecting with and utilizing the amazing speed, power, and agility of our subconscious minds, we can begin to use the Law of Attraction in a deliberate way to more effectively attract and create the results we desire.

> *Within you right now is the power*
> *to do things you never dreamed possible.*
> *This power becomes available to you*
> *just as soon as you can change*
> *your beliefs.*
>
> *Dr. Maxwell Maltz*

Our subconscious mind can take us wherever want to go, and
help us reach our goals in life much faster . . . and much faster
than our conscious mind.

(4)

EMOTIONS

Your emotions are the key.

Your emotions are a critical component in the application of
the Law of Attraction. Learn to listen to them—they are an
important internal feedback system that tells you of your
body's visceral response to the vibrational state you are creating.
You are creating this vibrational frequency with *whatever* you
are giving your attention to—the thoughts you are thinking,
the beliefs you are contemplating, the television show you are
watching, the music you are listening to, the book you are
reading, with *whatever activity* you are engaged in.

Your feelings are part of your internal guidance system. When
you are feeling joy and a sense of expansion, it simply means
you are *on course*—the things you are focusing on, the
thoughts you are thinking or creating, the ideas you are
entertaining, and the activities you are engaged in are actively
moving you in the direction of your purpose, dreams, and
desires.

When you are feeling anger, sadness, depression, and
hopelessness—any feelings that give you a sense of physical
contraction—then you are thinking thoughts and attending to
things that are *not* taking you toward your purpose, dreams,
or desires. This is feedback that is saying that you are *off
course*. Your emotions are telling you that it's time to switch
gears. They are telling you that it's time to think a more

uplifting thought, change your focus, change the channel, change the topic of discussion, and go do something different that will shift your energy and bring you feelings of joy and expansion.

> *Love is life.*
> *And if you miss love,*
> *you miss life.*
>
> Leo Buscaglia

Since your vibrational state is what attracts the objects of your desire, it is imperative to keep your emotions as positive as possible. Strive to keep your emotions in the positive range—feelings like joy, love, happiness, exhilaration, satisfaction, relief, pride, appreciation, relaxation, and serenity.

These feelings will raise your vibrational level and create a "vibrational match" for the experiences that you expect to have when your dreams do come to fruition. Remember, like attracts like. That which is like unto itself is drawn. So, by deliberately creating the positive emotional states that match the feelings we will have on the completion and fulfillment of our goals and desires, we are creating an energy field that will attract what we want. This is also why learning to respond to circumstances instead of just reacting to them, and thereby managing your emotional moods, is so important.

So, do the things that make you feel good—be passionate and enthusiastic about your life! When you feel emotions fully and deeply, you radiate more intense frequencies into the universe. The stronger and more intense your feelings are, the more accelerated the process of vibrational attraction becomes.

It is absolutely essential that you find the time to do the things that you love to do and take care of yourself in this way—no matter how busy your life already is.

Researchers are discovering that what you are *feeling* is actually far more important than what you are thinking or saying. *Your emotions never lie.* They are the true indicator of the thoughts you are having and whether or not you are acting in accordance with your personal truth, your heartfelt desires. Don't ignore them or try to reason your feelings away. First, just notice them. If they are not in the positive range (hope, expectation, acceptance, appreciation, love, and joy), either release them or simply choose a *better* thought. This means choosing a thought that creates a better feeling, or simply changing what it is that you are doing, and doing something that you enjoy instead. Go for a walk, put some music on, pet the cat, take charge and do *something* to shift you back into this positive range of emotions!

> *Everything you see happening is the*
> *consequence of that which you are.*
> David R. Hawkins

Internal and external feedback.

Remember, joy is your internal guidance system. It is your very own personal *internal feedback* device. If you are feeling excited, happy, and joyful, then chances are that you are on the right track, living in alignment with your personal truth. If you are feeling depressed, sad, or miserable, you probably are not. It's as simple as that. When you are in a state of joy or happiness, you are doing something right, so keep doing it. Pay attention to how you are feeling, and keep your compass heading set for "joy." Your happiness at this very moment is the key to attracting more happiness in the future.

Now, in addition to this internal feedback, you are also constantly receiving *external feedback*—messages from the universe. This feedback comes in many forms. It consists of the subtle and not so subtle signals that you get from other people, situations, and events in your life. You have surely experienced those times when things just seem to "click," and everything comes together for you smoothly and effortlessly. You feel supported in your actions and endeavors. This is *external feedback* telling you that you are *on course*.

In stark contrast, there are times when you meet resistance at every turn, and nothing seems to go well, no matter how hard you try. This is the universe providing external feedback to protect you and let you know that you are *off course*. You are swimming upstream, against the current. These internal and external feedback systems will let you know when you are on the right path and when you are on the wrong one. You simply need to learn to pay attention to what they are telling you. They will guide you, if you let them.

> *Every time I've done*
> *something that doesn't feel*
> *right, it's ended up*
> *not being right.*
>
> Mario Cuomo

Naturally, there will be times in our lives when sadness, grief, and sorrow are present. There is a natural ebb and flow in life, and without the lows, we would not appreciate the highs. Without the darkness, we would not appreciate the light. These painful times are often highly underrated opportunities for emotional and spiritual growth. They can provide us with a much needed frame of reference and help us by contrast and comparison to recognize and appreciate the many blessings in our lives.

It is obviously more difficult to keep our thoughts and feelings positive in the face of pain and darkness. Just know that you *do* have a choice about how you respond to or perceive any situation. There really are no "good" or "bad" events in our lives; we just have our own preconceived ideas and perceptions about certain things that make them so for us. *Everything* that happens in our lives provides an opportunity to grow in some way. Try to remember that any seemingly negative event can also become the seed of something beautiful and beneficial.

> *There are no mistakes, no coincidences.*
> *All events are blessings given to us*
> *to learn from.*
> Elisabeth Kübler-Ross

Positive and negative emotions.

You may have noticed that when you are feeling grateful, happy, or joyful there is a sense of lightness and expansion. You feel connected. You feel *alive!* This is your natural state of being. *This is what your life was intended to be.* Strive to live in a state of joy, wonder, and gratitude. These expansive positive emotions feel good and raise your vibrational frequency. In this place of love and joy, you are one with God, and you are a magnet for all of the beauty and abundance that the world has to offer.

Negative emotions, on the other hand, such as hatred, anger, jealousy, and fear create the opposite effect. They lower your vibrational frequency and make you feel anxious, tense, and constricted. They can create physical ailments and disease. Negative emotions invariably create a sense of separation, a feeling of disconnection. They are like a stone wall—a barrier to the joy that is who you really are. These emotions will effectively block the flow of positive energy into your life and will only serve to attract more negative energy.

So, if you have been holding onto feelings of anger, fear, resentment, or betrayal, now is the time to let them go. Release those old thoughts and patterns of behavior, and start living in the present. By focusing on your pain or anger, you are only drawing even more negative and unhealthy circumstances into your life. You need to make room for the positive feelings and experiences that you want to attract.

Anger makes you smaller,
while forgiveness forces you to
grow beyond what you were.

Cherie Carter-Scott

Forgiveness.

The act of forgiveness is a necessary and truly transformational process. You must be willing to forgive any person or situation that has caused you pain, and release them. By hanging on to old negative thoughts and emotions you are only harming yourself and attracting even more negative energy. It's been said that when you are unwilling to forgive someone, it's like drinking poison and waiting for the *other* person to get sick! So, just bless the person or the situation and wish them well. Forgive them, let them go, and be willing to forgive yourself as well, if need be.

By acknowledging your positive past and releasing your negative past—you can make room for a beautiful future. True forgiveness is extremely cathartic—it will cleanse you and set you free. It is an incredibly powerful process, one that will immediately shift you from a place of pain and anger to a higher vibrational frequency of love.

If you haven't forgiven yourself something,
how can you expect to forgive others?

Dolores Huerta

Since the Law of Attraction responds to the energy vibration of your thoughts and emotions, you need to focus your attention on the things that bring you into a state of positive vibration. Many experts on the Law of Attraction say that nothing is more important than *feeling good*. So, find the time to do the things that bring you joy and make you happy. Listen to the music you love. Take a walk on the beach. Do something nice for someone else. Treat yourself well. Make a conscious decision to choose thoughts that are positive and to be a vibrational match for what you want to attract into your life. Be intentional and deliberate in your creation of positive feelings and circumstances, and the universe will respond accordingly.

*You must bring yourself into
alignment with what you are asking for.
That's what joy is, that's what appreciation is,
that's what the feeling of passion is.
But when you are feeling despair,
or fear, or anger, those are strong indicators
that you are not right now in alignment
with what you are asking for.*

Esther Hicks

Remember, nobody else can tell you how to feel. Only you can make that decision. If you find yourself feeling bad, then you need to look at what is creating the negative feelings—it's not the external things, it's *you*, and the judgments, beliefs, ideas, and thoughts you have about those external things. So, the way you choose to *perceive* a situation will determine your emotional response, and you can deliberately choose to see anything and everything in a positive light.

You must make a conscious decision to *choose* happiness. Choose optimism. Choose to live in a place of constant gratitude and joy.

Settle for nothing less than magnificence in your life. Your emotions fuel your energy, and your energy fuels your future.

Dwell not on the past.
Use it to illustrate a point, then leave it behind.
Nothing really matters except
what you do now in this instant of time.
From this moment onwards
you can be an entirely different person,
filled with love and understanding,
ready with an outstretched hand, uplifted and
positive in every thought and deed.
Eileen Caddy

(5)
FOCUS ON THE POSITIVE

Make a conscious decision to focus on the positive.

The Law of Attraction doesn't filter out the information we provide. It doesn't decide what is better for us. We have free will, and we decide where we want to focus our energy and our attention. The universe just reflects it back to us. If we focus our attention on something (either positively or negatively), it will simply respond with more of it.

So, it's really important to focus on what you *do* want, not on what you don't want. State your desires in a positive way. Your mind works in pictures, so if you say "I don't want to be mad," you are creating the picture and the vibration of being "mad." The universe only receives the frequency of "mad" and responds to that. You must focus on the *opposite* of what you don't want. In this case, it would be a better choice to say "I want to be more loving and accepting of the way things are."

> *Once you replace negative*
> *thoughts with positive ones, you'll*
> *start having positive results.*
>
> Willie Nelson

Basically, you need to avoid sending mixed signals to the universe and those around you. They will hinder your ability to attract and manifest in a clear and powerful way.

For example: When you are "against" something, you are actually recreating it. You are creating more of the very thing that you want to eliminate! If you are "antiwar," think again. The operative word here is "war," and that is exactly what you will get more of. A better choice is to be "propeace." The universe will receive the vibration of "peace" and respond accordingly. The war on terrorism has created more terrorism. Violence attracts violence, and love attracts more love.

Make this simple change in your life. Make a conscious effort to restructure the way you think and speak, and avoid giving any unnecessary energy to the things you don't want in your life. Whenever possible, avoid subjecting yourself, your thoughts, and your emotions to the negative people and influences in your life.

**We cannot become what we need
to be by remaining what we are.**

Max Depree

Be aware that negativity can be very insidious. It sneaks into our lives through the evening news and the daily paper. It is so commonplace that it almost seems normal—we have become nearly immune to our daily doses of war, crime, violence, and corruption. Make a stand here. Refuse to give it your attention. Refuse to give it your focus. You have to stop attending to the things you don't want. Stop talking about them, stop reading about them, and stop talking about how bad they are. *Focus only on what you want to attract more of.* Remember, where your attention goes, your energy flows.

It's not surprising that most of us have a tendency to phrase things in a negative way, without necessarily meaning to do so. It's simply a bad habit. Remember from this point on to focus only on what it is that you *do* want. Do this not only with your own internal thoughts, but in your communication with others, as well. Try to avoid the use of any limiting or negative language. Every single thought you have, and every word you speak, sends a message to the universe. You are continually placing your order for your future life experiences.

Try replacing your negative messages with positive ones.

Here are a few examples:

Instead of thinking "I don't want to be late,"
      think "I want to be on time."

Instead of thinking "I don't want to forget,"
      think "I want to remember."

Instead of thinking "I can't. . . ,"
      think "I am beginning to . . ."

Instead of saying "Don't slam the door,"
      say "Please close the door gently."

Instead of saying "Your room is a mess,"
      say "Please keep your room clean."

Instead of saying "Stop making so much noise,"
      say "Please be a little more quiet."

Think about this for a moment. If you tell someone "Don't knock that glass over, you'll spill the milk," what is the image that pops into your mind? Naturally, you envision a glass being knocked over and a puddle of milk. You need to avoid creating the thought, the picture, and the energy vibration of the thing you don't want . . . and stay focused on those thoughts and images that are in harmony with what you *do* want to create in your life. By doing so, you will also avoid implanting the image of what you don't want in the minds of others . . . and in the universal mind!

We have a tendency to focus on what we *don't* want in so many areas of our lives, even when it comes to our own health. Think of how often when faced with an illness or disease we become completely preoccupied with the problem and not the desired outcome. We tend to give our focus entirely to the illness, and all that it entails, instead of focusing on being healthy. Since what you focus on expands, you want to direct your energy and thoughts to those of being *well*. Keep your thoughts positive and optimistic, and see yourself as healthy and whole. Your positive energy, thoughts, visualizations, affirmations, prayer, and meditation combined with whatever medical treatment you choose to seek will serve to enhance the healing process. Remember, in *every* aspect of your life keep your focus as much as possible on what it is that you *do* want and not on that which you don't want.

The secret of health for both
mind and body is not to mourn for the past,
worry about the future, or anticipate troubles . . .
but to live in the present moment
wisely and earnestly.

Buddha

Think about how much time we typically spend each day discussing our problems and focusing on what's wrong with our lives. From now on, make a commitment to shift your energy, and start thinking and speaking in a more positive way. Make it a point to start focusing on what is *right* in your life!

Start paying attention to *where* your attention is going! You will be surprised to realize just how frequently you think, speak, or act with your focus inadvertently on the opposite of what you really want. Remember, you are always attracting something, so stop attracting what you don't want and start attracting what you do want. Direct your attention only to those things that are worthy of it and that are in direct alignment with your dreams and goals.

By the way, it's OK to *notice* what you don't want. Just use it as a first step in the process of deciding what you do want, and try to get out of the habit of giving it so much of your energy and attention. Think about what you *don't* want just long enough to help identify what it is that you *do* want. This will tell you by comparison what it is that you would *rather* have and help provide you with some clarity. Remember to redirect your focus back to the positive, and move on.

Become a vibrational match for the future you desire.
Focus on the good within yourself and others.
Focus on the light and the beauty in your life.

> *The person who sends out positive thoughts activates the world around him positively and draws back to him positive results.*
> Dr. Norman Vincent Peale

(6)
ABUNDANCE

Abundance is a natural state of being.

Anything you wish for can flow effortlessly into your life if you understand and apply the Law of Attraction. We live in a world that seems to emphasize scarcity and lack, and yet the truth is, this is an *abundant* universe. There is no scarcity, there is no lack. There is more than enough food, money, joy, happiness, spiritual fulfillment, and love for everyone.

If you want to create an abundance of love in your life, then *focus* on love. *Be* the love you want to attract. Become more loving and generous with others and with yourself. By creating the vibration of love, you will automatically draw more love into your life. Focus on whatever it is that you want to create more of in your life, and remember to be grateful for that which you already have. Gratitude itself is a form of abundance, and the vibrational frequency of gratitude and appreciation will automatically attract even more to be grateful for.

Abundance is not something we acquire.
It is something we tune into. There's no
scarcity of opportunity to make a living
at what you love. There is only a scarcity
of resolve to make it happen.

Wayne Dyer

For example: If you want to create financial abundance in your life, then start by *focusing* on prosperity and money flowing into your life. Envision the checks coming in the mail. Write yourself a check for the sum of money you wish to manifest this year, and post it in a visible location. Every time you see it, *believe* that it is possible. Make a donation to your favorite charity, and *know* that you can afford it. You must be willing to *give* in order to receive. Imagine just how amazing it will feel to have complete financial freedom. Envision the various things you will do, the places you will go, and how it will change your life. Really let yourself feel it as though it were already so. Now, think of how you will use your financial prosperity to contribute and give back within your community. Imagine how *good* it will feel to help others and to really make a difference in their lives. Remember to take a moment to be thankful for everything that you already have. By doing this, you are creating a vibrational match for the financial abundance that you want to attract into your future life.

Now, this doesn't mean that you shouldn't also take action. It simply means that in order to create and receive abundance in your life you must be willing to move toward your goals on an *internal* level as well as on an external level. You must be clear about your desires (in this case, financial abundance) believe it will happen, and as an extension of your belief, you must be willing to take all the normal logical action steps that make sense, along with any inspired actions that occur to you. You must be willing to follow your inspired impulses, maintain a vibrational match for what you want to attract, and trust that the results are already being created for you. You are no longer fighting the current, but moving effortlessly downstream with the natural rhythm and flow of life.

> *Whatever we are waiting for—peace of mind,*
> *contentment, grace, the inner awareness of*
> *simple abundance—it will surely come to us, but*
> *only when we are ready to receive it with*
> *an open and grateful heart.*
> Sarah Ban Breathnach

The entire universe will support you abundantly in *every* way when you are moving with this kind of purpose and intention in the direction of your dreams. It will respond to the vibration of your passion and commitment. So, start paying attention to the many synchronicities in your life and become aware of all the opportunities, ideas, people, and resources that you are attracting. Be open to them, and be willing to think outside the box. New opportunities will often present themselves in surprising ways. Do what you love to do, be passionate about it, and believe in yourself.

If you are willing to invest yourself wholeheartedly in your dreams, then all the necessary resources, including the money, will follow.

There is no order of difficulty in the universe; and there is no scarcity of money in the world. If you are currently in debt, then figure out a payment plan, commit to it, and then shift your focus away from the debt, and start focusing on the wealth you are creating instead.

> *Not what we have but what we enjoy*
> *constitutes our abundance.*
>
> John Petit-Senn

Basically, the universe will respond abundantly to the vibration of *whatever* you are passionate about, focused upon, committed to, and to that which you truly believe is possible. Whatever you focus on expands, so don't allow yourself to entertain any limiting thoughts or beliefs. Focus your thoughts, feelings, and energy instead on expansiveness and on the unlimited possibilities before you. Use the power of your conscious and subconscious mind to create a vibrational match for the abundance you desire and deserve.

Be sure to also take the time to appreciate all of the amazing abundance that is already present in your life, and open yourself up to receiving *all* the good that the universe has to offer. Through the Law of Attraction, the universe will respond to the vibration of your sincere gratitude and appreciation with even greater abundance.

Use the Law of Attraction to attract abundance in *every* area of your life. This is an abundant universe. There are no limits. Just as the ocean doesn't care if you come to it with a thimble, a cup, a bucket, or a tank car for water, neither does the universe.

Abundant love, joy, health, wealth, and happiness are yours for the asking.
They are your natural right.
All you have to do is claim them.

You can have anything you want
if you want it badly enough. You can be anything
you want to be, do anything you set out to
accomplish if you hold to that desire with
singleness of purpose.
Abraham Lincoln

(7)

PURPOSE AND PASSION

Find your purpose and passion in life.

Each one of us is born with a unique life purpose. We are all here for a reason, and we are all here to serve each other. We are like individual cells in a body, each of us performing our own unique functions and collectively serving the being as a whole. A life of purpose is not only a true expression of who you really are—it is your gift to the world—and the world needs what you have to offer. When you are living your life "on purpose," you will find greater fulfillment and joy in all that you do. The universe will support you in all of your endeavors when you are living in alignment with your purpose, your passion, and your inner truth.

> *The purpose of life is to live a life of purpose.*
> *Richard Leider*

So, you must take the time to look deeply within yourself and identify your own personal mission and purpose in life. This is best done through quiet contemplation, prayer, and meditation, but there are a few things that you can do right now to get started. You can begin by internalizing the fact that there are no accidents, and that you are indeed here on the planet for a reason. You have a purpose in this life and in this world, and your contribution matters.

Most of us are not really quite clear about what our purpose is—we haven't really taken the time to search our souls and discover our true calling. We've gotten sidetracked with bills, responsibilities, work, and too little spare time to even find out what it is that we really enjoy. This is a compromise to who you really are and what you have to offer the world. You *must* give priority to discovering your real mission in life. You are not living to your fullest potential or contributing to your fullest abilities unless you are living a life of purpose.

> *Your true passion*
> *should feel like breathing;*
> *it's that natural.*
> Oprah Winfrey

Here's how it works. You've been given clues to your purpose throughout your entire life. You have your own completely unique gifts, talents, interests, strengths, and qualities—*and you are meant to use them*. The things that bring you the greatest joy in life and make you feel really alive are another clue to your purpose. So, what it boils down to is really quite simple: you are meant to do what brings you joy, and your gifts and talents are meant to be your contribution to the world. A life lived with purpose and intention is one that will honor and nourish your spirit on the deepest level while simultaneously contributing to the world around you.

Defining your purpose.

Take a few moments of still, quiet time to clear your mind of any distractions. The techniques below are a way to logically begin the process of defining your purpose, but you will ultimately want to answer these questions from a deeper place of consciousness through prayer and meditation, as well.

Start by making a list of all the times you can remember in your life that have made you feel the most *truly alive and joyful*.

The times I have felt the most alive and joyful:

_____

_____

_____

_____

_____

_____

_____

_____

_____

_____

_____

_____

_____

Look closely at this list, and ask yourself what each of these experiences has in common. Make note of it. This common element is an indication of what brings you joy . . . and what brings you joy is an indication of your life purpose!

Now, consider the following questions, and write down your answers.

What are my natural gifts?

_____

_____

_____

_____

_____

_____

_____

What are my skills and talents?

_____

_____

_____

_____

_____

_____

_____

What do I love to do?

_____

_____

_____

_____

_____

_____

_____

When do I feel the most alive?

_____

_____

_____

_____

_____

_____

_____

What am I passionate about?

_____

_____

_____

_____

_____

_____

_____

_____

What brings me the greatest joy in life?

_____

_____

_____

_____

_____

_____

_____

_____

When do I feel the best about myself ?

_____

_____

_____

_____

_____

_____

_____

_____

_____

What are my personal strengths and characteristics?

_____

_____

_____

_____

_____

_____

_____

_____

_____

What have others always said that I am really good at?

_____

_____

_____

_____

_____

_____

_____

How do I most enjoy interacting with other people?

_____

_____

_____

_____

_____

_____

_____

What would I change in the world if I could?

_____

_____

_____

_____

_____

_____

_____

_____

What are the common characteristics of your answers to all of these questions?

What do these answers have in common with the list you made earlier?

Ask through prayer or meditation for clarity, divine guidance, and inspiration. Ask to be shown how you can best use your gifts and the joyful places within yourself to not only earn a living, but to be of service to the world.

Now, take your answers from these questions and your list and consolidate them into two or three complete sentences. You are in the process of defining your life purpose—your personal mission statement based upon who you authentically are and your unique interests, gifts, talents, and passions.

My life purpose.

_____

_____

_____

_____

_____

_____

_____

_____

_____

_____

_____

_____

_____

_____

_____

_____

_____

By creating your life purpose statement you are defining who you are, who you want to be, and how you want to show up in the world. Now, open your mind and your heart to the possibilities that already exist. Listen for the answers to your prayers, and become aware of the ideas, inspiration, and opportunities that present themselves.

Things will begin to unfold for you as exactly as they are meant to—and within the timeframe that will serve your highest good. Follow your inspired thoughts and ideas, and *dream big*. You don't have to know exactly how to turn your mission statement into reality yet—once you have defined your purpose, just be open to the various possibilities that arise for you. Be willing to let go, and let God.

> *If you want to be happy, set a goal*
> *that commands your thoughts,*
> *liberates your energy,*
> *and inspires your hope.*
>
> Andrew Carnegie

Whenever you are doing what you love and are passionate about, the universe will automatically respond through the Law of Attraction and support you in every way. Imagine your life and your work filled with meaning, purpose, and passion! Imagine how good it feels to do what you love, have fun doing it, make money *and* make a significant difference in the world.

The happiest and most successful people in life are those who have managed to structure their careers and activities around their gifts and passions in life. By doing so, they have attracted all of the ideas, resources, people, and finances that were needed to create the lives of their dreams. They have created a vibrational match for joy and abundance in their lives by identifying their purpose, believing in their dreams, and moving forward confidently in the direction of their goals and desires.

Start living consciously and "on purpose." Everything that you do, every activity that you participate in, should be in alignment with your joy, your higher truth, and your mission in life. Don't withhold your true gifts and talents from the world any longer. A life lived with purpose and intention is one that is fulfilling on every level. Work is meant to be fun, life is meant to be fun, and the world needs what you have to offer! You were put on this earth for a reason, and you must begin to honor that reason. Let *all* that you do flow from your purpose and passion, and you will experience (and attract) true happiness, abundance, and success.

Create a life filled with passion and significance.
Create a life of purpose.
Follow your bliss.

*There is one quality that one must possess
to win, and that is definiteness of purpose,
the knowledge of what one wants,
and a burning desire to possess it.*

Napoleon Hill

(8)

DEFINE YOUR DREAMS

What are your dreams?

Give deep thought to what you want to create in your life. Consider each of the various areas of your life and focus on what you *do* want, not what you don't. Get in touch with your inner truth, your authentic dreams, goals, and your heartfelt desires. Honor these and own them without fear, shame, or inhibition. Your dreams and desires are not subject to anyone else's approval. They are yours and yours alone, but you have to define them in order to achieve them.

You deserve to have whatever you truly want in your life, and all of your dreams are valid if they are important to you. It doesn't matter if your dream is a romantic relationship, a new car, a new skill, a vacation, or financial prosperity. By the way, contrary to popular belief, there is nothing wrong with desiring financial wealth. You can do a lot of good in the world with greater financial assets in the bank. It is only the *attachment* to money that can become problematic, so just remember that you must give in order to receive, and keep your intentions high.

Your dreams and aspirations should serve to ignite the passion within you, and this passion will not only inspire you to achieve them, it will also send a positive vibrational frequency out into the world. Naturally, through the Law of Attraction, the universe will respond accordingly.

Remember that *all* things are possible. Don't limit or censor your visions for the future. You must believe in yourself and believe that you are worthy. Keep all of your actions, dreams, goals, and desires in alignment with your life purpose. Decide what you *really* want your future to look like.

> *We've got to have a dream*
> *if we are going to make*
> *a dream come true.*
> Denis Waitley

There are seven important areas in your life that you will want to consider as you begin to define your goals and dreams.

Seven key areas in life:

Personal goals (things you want to do, be, and have . . .)

Relationships (friends, family, romantic, coworkers . . .)

Health and Body (wellness, fitness, body image . . .)

Career & Education (job, school, career goals . . .)

Recreation (sports, hobbies, fun, vacations . . .)

Financial (income, savings, investments . . .)

Contribution (charities, community service . . .)

Do you have any idea what your personal goals and aspirations really are? Have you identified your life purpose? What is it that you love to do? What are you passionate about? What do you want to accomplish? Where do you want to go? What do you want to be? How can you give to others? What causes speak to you? What are your intentions?

Unfortunately, most of us have given very little time or thought to these questions. We've gotten so caught up in the hustle and bustle of our daily routines that we just haven't taken the time. We're pretty good at itemizing the things that *haven't* been going so well and the things we have to complain about. So, we're pretty clear about what we *don't* want, but we haven't given much consideration to what we *do* want. In order to attract what you want in your life, you must first take the time to clearly identify your dreams and desires.

> ***To the person who does not know***
> ***where he wants to go there is***
> ***no favorable wind.***
> *Seneca*

Think of it like this. When you go into your local Starbucks® and place your order, do you say "I *don't* want tea," or "I *don't* want an espresso," or "I *don't* want cappuccino?" Of course not! You place your order for a tall, nonfat mocha, easy chocolate, extra whipped cream with total clarity and specificity—and the absolute confidence that you will get exactly what you ordered.

To operate in harmony with the Law of Attraction, you must place your order for life in much the same way. *You need to clarify your goals, and be specific.* Stop settling for whatever just happens to come your way in life, and take ownership of the fact that you can actively participate in the creation of your own future by clearly stating your desires.

The bottom line is, if you don't really know exactly what you are asking for, then how can you expect to get it? So, it is imperative that you take the time to decide what you really want to attract in your life, write it down, and be perfectly clear about it.

> *You must see your goals clearly and specifically before you can set out for them. Hold them in your mind until they become second nature.*
>
> Les Brown

Create your dream list.

Your dream list will be a comprehensive overview of your dreams, goals and desires. It will represent what you want to be, do, have, and achieve in all areas of your life. Later on you will want to prioritize your list and focus your attention on certain areas, but for now it is best to go ahead and look at the bigger picture. There are a few techniques you can use to help you identify your desires and clarify your goals.

The first technique is the creation of "T-chart." This type of chart (see the example we have provided) is a very effective way to identify what you *do* want in your life by looking just briefly at the things you *don't* want. Consider each of the seven key areas of your life. Address one area or subject at a time, such as career, personal goals, or relationships, and decide what your particular topic within that area is. For instance, within the relationship category of your life you may want to focus on a topic such as "My Ideal Romantic Relationship" and start by writing down what you don't want in that area of your life in one column, and then in another column turn it around into an *opposite* statement, saying what it is that you *do* want.

I suggest creating a T-chart for *each* area of your life and listing what it is that you don't want on the left side, then listing what you do want on the right side, stated in a *positive* way. There are charts for each area of your life on the pages to follow.

By the way, this is an example of it being okay to start by noticing what you don't want. In order to really clarify what you *do* want to attract into your life, it is often helpful to take a brief look at what you *don't* want.

Here's an example of this type of chart:

SUBJECT: relationships	My ideal romantic relationship
What I don't want	What I do want
Someone who watches TV all weekend	Someone who enjoys an active lifestyle
A smoker or a drinker	Someone who cares about their health
An angry or abusive person	A kind and compassionate person

Use the charts that appear on the following pages for each of the seven areas in your life. This will help you clarify your goals and desires. When you have completed them, go back and *cross off the "don't want" list on the left side of each chart*. From now on, just use the right side of each list and stay focused on what you *do* want in your life. There is no need to give any further attention or energy to the list of what you don't want. By the way, the simple act of crossing out what you don't want is empowering, and it feels good!

When you are finished, combine the lists of what you *do* want into one single list. You can use the Dream List pages we have provided, or use a separate piece of paper. Be sure to write out your dreams and goals in complete sentences, and leave some room for expansion.

This is the beginning of your dream list! By filling in these pages, you will be one step closer to achieving them.

Clarity is power.

Buckminster Fuller

You will want to be thorough when you make your dream list. For instance, you don't want to get the house of your dreams only to realize that you can't afford the mortgage—and you forgot to really specify your financial goals . . . so be as specific and comprehensive as possible. Once you are finished, there are a few more questions that you might want to consider when defining your dreams, so take a few minutes to review the questions on page 76, and make any appropriate additions to your dream list.

Here are charts for each of the seven key areas in your life and your Dream List:

SUBJECT:

Personal goals

What I don't want	What I do want

SUBJECT:

Personal goals

What I don't want	What I do want

SUBJECT:

Relationships

What I don't want	What I do want

SUBJECT:

Relationships

What I don't want	What I do want

SUBJECT:

Health and Body

What I don't want	What I do want

SUBJECT:

Health and Body

What I don't want	What I do want

SUBJECT:

Career & Education

What I don't want	What I do want

SUBJECT:

Career & Education

What I don't want	What I do want

SUBJECT:

Recreation

What I don't want	What I do want

SUBJECT:

Recreation

What I don't want	What I do want

SUBJECT:

Financial

What I don't want	What I do want

SUBJECT:

Financial

What I don't want	What I do want

SUBJECT:

Contribution

What I don't want	What I do want

SUBJECT:

Contribution

What I don't want	What I do want

My Dream List

_____

_____

_____

_____

_____

_____

_____

_____

_____

_____

_____

_____

_____

_____

_____

_____

_____

page 1

My Dream List

_____

_____

_____

_____

_____

_____

_____

_____

_____

_____

_____

_____

_____

_____

_____

_____

_____

page 2

My Dream List

_____

_____

_____

_____

_____

_____

_____

_____

_____

_____

_____

_____

_____

_____

_____

_____

_____

page 3

Now, ask yourself the following questions:

- ❖ What is my life purpose?
- ❖ What are my dreams?
- ❖ What are my goals?
- ❖ What am I grateful for?
- ❖ What makes me happy?
- ❖ How would I like to grow personally?
- ❖ How would I like to grow spiritually?
- ❖ What would my perfect relationship look like?
- ❖ What would my ideal family life consist of?
- ❖ What is something that I've always wanted to do?
- ❖ What would I like more of in my life?
- ❖ What would I like to *do* more of in my life?
- ❖ Where would I like to travel?
- ❖ Where would I like to live?
- ❖ What would my dream home be like?
- ❖ What career would I ideally choose or create for myself?
- ❖ What are my financial goals?
- ❖ How can I give back within my community?
- ❖ Which causes or charities would I like to be more involved with?
- ❖ If I could change the world, how would I make it a better place?

The questions on the previous page may inspire you and help you identify any additional dreams, goals, and desires. Take your time; give these questions some serious thought and consideration and add any of these responses that you wish to your dream list.

> *The first principle of success is desire—*
> *knowing what you want.*
> *Desire is the planting of the seed.*
>
> Robert Collier

101 Goals List.

There are no limits on your dreams and goals. The whole world is out there just waiting for you. This is an inspirational technique that you might want to try as well. A great process for clarifying some of your more long-term goals and dreams is to make a list of 101 goals that you would like to accomplish before you die—101 things you would like to do, be, or have.

At age fifteen, John Goddard, the world famous adventurer, made a list of 127 goals he wanted to achieve before he died. They included things like visiting the Great Pyramids, learning to scuba dive, seeing the Great Wall of China, climbing Mount Kilimanjaro, and reading the entire Encyclopedia of Britannica. He is now in his seventies, and he has achieved 109 of the goals on his list.

In his late twenties, Lou Holtz, the former football coach of Notre Dame, wrote down 108 goals that he wanted to achieve, including winning a national championship, eating dinner at the White House, meeting the pope, and landing a plane on an aircraft carrier. He is also in his seventies, and he has achieved 102 of his goals.

Inspired by both stories, I made a list of 109 goals seventeen years ago. So far, I have achieved sixty-three of those goals. The goals I have already achieved range from things like typing fifty words a minute to appearing in a movie, learning to ski and windsurf, writing a bestselling book, traveling to various exotic locations, buying my dream house, and having a syndicated newspaper column.

By writing down your own list of 101 goals (see chart on following pages) and reviewing your list every week or so, you will activate the Law of Attraction to set up the circumstances that will help you to achieve them. You will begin to notice all kinds of seemingly miraculous events occurring in your life. Some goals will take you longer to achieve than others, but they can all eventually come true. This list of lifetime goals may inspire some additions to your dream list, as well.

You are successful
the moment you start moving
toward a worthwhile goal.

Chuck Carlson

By the way, if your goals and dreams benefit others, as well as yourself, then the vibration of your intention resonates at a higher frequency. Think of ways to contribute to your family, friends, and community. Be open to finding a cause that really speaks to you personally, and get involved in it. Start tithing with your time and your donations. And because we really *are* all connected, your commitment to others is also a commitment to yourself.

As you achieve the various goals on your 101 goal list, you will want to highlight them, or note the date of your accomplishment. This act alone is empowering, and it is also a way to acknowledge the Law of Attraction at work in your life.

My 101 goals:

1. _____
   _____

2. _____
   _____

3. _____
   _____

4. _____
   _____

5. _____
   _____

6. _____
   _____

7. _____
   _____

8. _____
   _____

9. _____
   _____

10. _____
    _____

11. _____
    _____

12. _____
    _____

13. _____
    _____

My 101 goals:

14. _____
_____

15. _____
_____

16. _____
_____

17. _____
_____

18. _____
_____

19. _____
_____

20. _____
_____

21. _____
_____

22. _____
_____

23. _____
_____

24. _____
_____

25. _____
_____

26. _____
_____

My 101 goals:

27. _____
    _____

28. _____
    _____

29. _____
    _____

30. _____
    _____

31. _____
    _____

32. _____
    _____

33. _____
    _____

34. _____
    _____

35. _____
    _____

36. _____
    _____

37. _____
    _____

38. _____
    _____

39. _____
    _____

My 101 goals:

40. _____
_____

41. _____
_____

42. _____
_____

43. _____
_____

44. _____
_____

45. _____
_____

46. _____
_____

47. _____
_____

48. _____
_____

49. _____
_____

50. _____
_____

51. _____
_____

52. _____
_____

My 101 goals:

53. _____
    _____

54. _____
    _____

55. _____
    _____

56. _____
    _____

57. _____
    _____

58. _____
    _____

59. _____
    _____

60. _____
    _____

61. _____
    _____

62. _____
    _____

63. _____
    _____

64. _____
    _____

65. _____
    _____

My 101 goals:

66. _____

67. _____

68. _____

69. _____

70. _____

71. _____

72. _____

73. _____

74. _____

75. _____

76. _____

77. _____

My 101 goals:

78. _____

79. _____

80. _____

81. _____

82. _____

83. _____

84. _____

85. _____

86. _____

87. _____

88. _____

89. _____

My 101 goals:

90. _____
_____

91. _____
_____

92. _____
_____

93. _____
_____

94. _____
_____

95. _____
_____

96. _____
_____

97. _____
_____

98. _____
_____

99. _____
_____

100. _____
_____

101. _____
_____

By now you should have a really well rounded dream list going. You have looked at your specific goals in each area of your life, and you've looked at goals for the course of your lifetime. You've identified your purpose and your dreams, clearly stating what you want to create in your life. Some of your goals may be short-term goals, like losing twenty-five pounds or taking a vacation in Italy. Others may be more long term, such as transforming the educational system, increasing environmental awareness in your community, or becoming a millionaire.

Prioritize Your Dream List.

Take a few minutes now to prioritize your list. Think about which goals and dreams best support your personal mission statement, and which ones are of the most importance to you at this time in your life. Highlight or underline those items. *Concentrate your focus for right now on just these particular goals and dreams—the ones that you want to work on first.* Your focused thoughts and energy will facilitate the manifestation of those specific goals and dreams.

You will come back to the rest of your list—and the sheer act of creating the list has already sent a message to the universe—but start with the things that mean the most to you at this point in time. Remember that your dreams and goals may change and evolve over the years—and as you continue to grow and achieve more, your goals will probably grow as well.

Dream Big.

Don't censor your dreams or vision with practicalities and probabilities. You don't *need* to know every single step that it will take to achieve your goals. Just decide what you want. Know that you deserve it. Believe you can have it, then release it, and let it go. Open yourself up to infinite possibilities. Watch the miracles unfold.

Now, consider this possibility—if you can figure it all out on your own, then your dream may not be big enough!

You have created your dream list.
You have placed your order with the universe.
It is your written request for the future.

> *All our dreams can come true—*
> *if we have the courage to pursue them.*
> *Walt Disney*

(9)

LIVING THE LAW OF ATTRACTION

The first step in living the Law of Attraction is to understand how it works in our lives.

In the previous chapters we've discussed not only the Law of Attraction and the way it works in our lives, but we've also taken a look at who we are, what we are, our connection to universal source, and the role we have played in creating our lives up until now. We've taken a look at just how powerful our thoughts and emotions are. We've discussed the importance of releasing the negative and staying in a *positive* emotional state of attraction in order to be a vibrational match for our dreams and desires. We've acknowledged the amazing agility of our own subconscious mind and the importance of utilizing its unlimited potential to help us attract and create the lives we have only dreamed of in the past. We have also taken the time to define our purpose, dreams, and goals, and to clarify what it is that we want to attract in our lives.

Now that you understand a little bit more about how you participate in the process of the Law of Attraction, you can begin to take responsibility for everything that you are currently in the process of attracting into your life. Now that you are aware of the role you play in creating your life, *you can no longer create your future accidentally or by default!* Take this to heart, because *this* is your moment, your time to begin consciously, intentionally, and deliberately participating in the creation of the future you desire.

By now you have a pretty good idea of who you are, who you want to be, and where you want to go in life. You have a clear vision of what it is you want to do, be, and have. You actually have a desired outcome, a destination in mind now, and it is this desired outcome that you will want to focus on. It's a lot like programming an internal G.P.S. system to your chosen destination. Now that you know where you want to go, the universe will guide you there through the Law of Attraction.

> *Create your future*
> *from your future,*
> *not your past.*
> Werner Erhard

Tools for living the Law of Attraction.

In the chapters to follow, we will look at various methods and tools that will help you create and maintain a constant state of joy and positive energy. We will address several techniques for stimulating and strengthening your connection to your subconscious mind and inspiring your positive thoughts and emotions. In this section we will also discuss prayer and meditation, affirmations, visualization, attitude, appreciation, action, and faith. We will address how to actively become a vibrational match for what you want to draw into your life.

These tools and techniques will help you to make any necessary changes in your life, and they will help you to harness the power of your subconscious mind, as well as the power of the universe.

It's time to internalize your new positive emotions, thought patterns, and beliefs. It's time to really *see* the future you desire, *feel* the emotions it evokes, and *believe* that it is possible.

It's time to begin living the Law of Attraction.
It's time to begin living the life of your dreams.

> *To accomplish great things, we must not*
> *only act, but also dream,*
> *not only plan, but also believe.*
>
> Anatole France

(10)
AFFIRMATIONS

Affirmations are one of the most powerful ways to create a vibrational match for what you want to attract into your life.

Every thought you think and every word you say is an affirmation. Your thoughts and words are declarations of who you think you are and how you perceive the world to be. Every time you think a negative thought or make a self-deprecating comment you are actually affirming it as your personal truth. Fortunately, the same holds true for positive thoughts and statements.

Strong, positive affirmations are powerful means of self-transformation and they are a key element in the creation of the life you desire. They work by purposely replacing the limiting ideas, negative beliefs, and self-talk that you have taken on and internalized over the years with positive statements that assert who you want to be and how you want to experience life.

The goal here is to create positive, self-affirming, self-empowering statements that uplift and inspire you—that raise your emotional set point. There are two types of affirmations that we will be addressing: *positive affirmations* and *goal specific affirmations*.

First say to yourself what you would be
and then do what you have to do.

Epictetus

Positive affirmations

Positive affirmations simply affirm your positive beliefs about yourself and about life.

Examples of positive affirmations:

My life is abundant in every way.
I am successful in all that I do.
My life is filled with love and beauty.
I am grateful for each experience in my life.
I am divinely guided and protected.
I am attracting joy into my life.
I am excited to be alive!
I believe all things are possible.
I am loved.
I can do anything.
I make a difference in this world.

These simple declarations of who you want to be and how you want to feel are extremely powerful, and they help to replace the negative, limiting beliefs that you may have taken on in the past. Those old negative subconscious thoughts are actually reprogrammed through the use of these positive affirmations into strong positive feelings and images.

You will want to create your own positive affirmations and use them on a daily basis. We have created a place for you to write them down on the pages to follow. All of your affirmations will work best when they are read and repeated several times a day. Be consistent—it usually takes about thirty days to reprogram your thought patterns. Say your positive affirmations out loud with feeling, and experience the emotions they evoke for you.

> *Constant repetition*
> *carries conviction.*
> *Robert Collier*

For even more powerful results, you can repeat them while making eye contact with yourself in the mirror. Affirm just how wonderful you are and how great your life is. Feel it, believe it, and fully receive it in all of your being. You are recreating your self-image, building positive attitudes, and internalizing a more positive belief system.

Goal specific affirmations

Goal specific affirmations affirm your specific dreams, desires, and goals as having already been completed.

These affirmations are statements that describe a goal in its already completed state, such as "I am celebrating feeling light and alive in my perfect body weight of 135." These affirmations will help you to create the emotional experience of having already attracted what it is that you want. The feelings of joy, happiness, exhilaration, excitement, confidence, relief, inner peace, and so on, are the vibrational match for the physical manifestation that you want to attract.

> *Every thought we think*
> *is creating our future.*
> *Louise L. Hay*

These affirmations create a positive expectation that you *will* achieve these goals, and they increase your desire and motivation to act on these goals and dreams.

In addition to that, they actually do something pretty amazing. They begin to literally *reprogram* the reticular activating system in your brain, so that you will start to become more aware of people, money, resources, and ideas that will help you achieve your goals. These resources were always present, but your brain was actually filtering them out. Through the regular use of your affirmations you will reprogram the filter and expand your perception and awareness.

Here are a few guidelines for creating your own goal specific affirmations:

Affirmations are positive.

Avoid using the word "not" in an affirmation.

Affirmations are stated in the present tense.
   (Believe it is already so.)

Affirmations are fairly short.

Affirmations are specific.

Begin your affirmations with "I am . . ." or "we are . . ."

Affirmations use action words. *(Feel the emotions when you say the affirmation.)*

Affirmations are personal. *(Make affirmations for your own behavior, not other's.)*

**Here are a few examples
of goal specific affirmations:**

❖ I am feeling exhilarated and alive,
snowboarding down the mountain face
on this perfect winter day.

❖ I am feeling proud as I stand looking at
the house that I have helped to build for
Habitat for Humanity.

❖ I am excitedly watching orders pour in
over the Internet for my new products.

❖ I am feeling so proud to be graduating at
the top of my class with honors.

❖ I am looking around me at the faces
of the children I am helping, and I am
thrilled to know that I have really made
a difference in their lives.

❖ I am thankfully receiving another
perfect bill of health from my doctor.

❖ I am feeling relaxed and grateful to be
sitting here on the beach in Hawaii with
my toes buried in the warm sand, feeling
the warmth of the sun on my face.

❖ I am thrilled to open the mailbox and
find that yet another check has arrived.

❖ I am happily watching my family as they
laugh and frolic in the snow.

- ❖ I am joyfully driving my new Lexus LS430 down Pacific Coast Highway.

- ❖ I am effectively communicating my needs and desires to my family.

- ❖ I am feeling joyful and content as I gaze lovingly into the eyes of my partner.

- ❖ I am happily stepping through the door of my brand new dream home.

It's not what is available
or unavailable that determines
your level of success and happiness;
it's what you convince
yourself is true.

Dr. Wayne Dyer

Now, go ahead and take a few minutes to develop your own positive and goal specific affirmations. Create strong personal affirmations that reinforce your positive beliefs and that will replace any of your negative self-talk with a strong positive statement. Use the charts on the following pages and write them down. You might want to refer to your dream list, too, and keep those desires and goals in mind as you write your goal specific affirmations.

MY POSITIVE AFFIRMATIONS

MY GOAL-SPECIFIC AFFIRMATIONS

How to use your affirmations:

1. Repeat your affirmations at least three times a day. The best times are first thing in the morning, the middle of the day, and around bedtime.

2. Work in depth with a *few* affirmations. This is much more effective than working less frequently with a greater number of them.

3. Say your affirmations out loud, if possible. If not, read them silently to yourself.

4. Close your eyes and visualize yourself as the affirmation describes. See the scene *through your eyes*, as if it were happening around you, just the way you would be seeing it in real life.

5. Hear the sounds; see the images that would be present when you successfully achieve what your affirmation describes. Include any other people who would be there, and hear their words of encouragement and congratulations.

6. Feel the emotions that you would experience when you achieve this goal. The stronger your feelings are, the more powerful the impact.

Repeat this entire process with each of your affirmations. You may also want to try writing your affirmations down on a piece of paper ten to twenty times each day. This is another powerful way to internalize them and imprint them in your subconscious mind.

We are what we repeatedly do.
Excellence then, is not an
action, but a habit.

Aristotle

By repeating and visualizing your affirmations in this way, you are maximizing the effect of each one and what it means to you personally. The Law of Attraction will respond to the energy of the thoughts, images, and feelings created by each affirmation, and your subconscious mind will respond by storing the new beliefs and treating them as reality. Remember, your subconscious mind can't tell the difference between what is real and what is vividly imagined.

If you find that negative or limiting responses, such as doubt or skepticism, keep emerging in your mind as you are saying your affirmations, then you may want to use one of the releasing techniques we referred to in chapter three. You can also create new affirmations that are the opposite of each of the negative thoughts and add these to your daily routine.

Make a commitment to use your affirmations every single day. Let them become a personal ritual, something you look forward to. *This* is how we reprogram ourselves: through repetition, association, and emotion. The level of emotional intensity that you feel while using your affirmations will determine the intensity of the attraction they create.

You are literally reprogramming your beliefs about yourself and the world you live in with each affirmation.

The thing you set your
mind on is the thing you
ultimately become.

Nathaniel Hawthorne

(11)

VISUALIZATION

**Your ability to visualize your dreams
will serve as a catalyst in their creation.**

Visualization exercises and techniques are incredibly powerful. Some psychologists are now claiming that one hour of visualization is worth seven hours of physical effort. Remember, your subconscious mind *cannot* tell the difference between a real experience and a vividly imagined experience. It can't differentiate between your remembering, pretending, or actually experiencing the event. It responds to all of them equally. Through various visualization techniques you can fully experience any situation as though it were real. You can create emotional and physiological responses to the situation you are visualizing. Your subconscious mind will internalize this information and store it as truth, and the universe will respond to this vibrational energy with the manifestation that matches it.

> *Visualization is daydreaming
> with a purpose.*
> Bo Bennett

Here is an example of a two part visualization exercise that paints a vivid picture in your mind and brings home the fact that your thoughts and emotions influence your body, as well.

As you read part one, notice how you feel emotionally and physically, and pay attention to how those feelings and sensations differ in part two of the example.

The Skyscraper Visualization.
Part One

> Take a deep breath and let yourself relax . . .
> Imagine that you are standing in the middle of a
> small terrace on the top of the tallest skyscraper
> in the entire world. Also, imagine that this
> terrace has no railing . . . there is nothing at all
> between you and that vertical drop. As you are
> standing there, look down at your feet and notice
> what the terrace is made out of. Are you standing
> on tile, concrete, asphalt, wood, or stone? Notice
> that the weather is nice. The sun is shining, there
> is a soft cool breeze, and you can feel the warmth
> of the sun on your face and your arms . . . what
> noises can you hear? Maybe there are some
> pigeons or other birds up there. Maybe you can
> hear a helicopter flying by or the street noises far
> below. . . . Now, walk out to the very edge of the
> terrace and put your toes right against the edge.
> Look down at the street far, far below . . . see how
> incredibly small everything appears to be from
> way up here. As you are doing this notice how
> you are feeling. . . . Now, slowly walk back to the
> center of the terrace . . . still remembering just
> how you felt when you were standing at the edge
> and looking down.

Most people will notice some type of emotional and physical reaction. You may have felt your heart racing, your palms sweating, dizziness, or nausea. You may have experienced a feeling of tension or fear.

Part Two

Take a deep breath and let yourself relax . . . imagine once more that you are standing on top of the same terrace, on top of the same sky-scraper as before, only this time you have beautiful white feathered wings, and you are totally confident in your ability to fly. You realize that you are totally safe. . . . So, let yourself walk to the edge of the terrace and when you get there, just gently bend your knees, push off, and fly. . . . Notice what it feels like to fly—feel the wind rushing beneath your wings as you soar and glide effortlessly through the sky . . . feel the exhilaration and the freedom. . . . After a while, let yourself fly to any place on the planet that you would really like to be right now. . . . It might be a favorite vacation spot, a place you like to go when you want to be alone, or a special place you would like to go to be with someone you care about. . . . When you get there, just let yourself gently land and spend a few moments enjoying yourself, doing whatever you would like to do there . . . notice how you feel right now, physically, and emotionally.

Compare the different emotional and physical reactions you felt in part one and part two of the visualization. Notice the lightness, joy, and sense of expansion you feel in part two of this example.

Now, think about this for a moment. You haven't gone anywhere, you haven't left the room, you've only taken a few minutes to visually *imagine* these two experiences, and yet you probably felt very distinct and different emotional and physiological changes occurring. The vivid images you created in your mind were completely real to your subconscious mind, and it responded to your imagined experiences on an emotional and physiological level as though they were actually occurring.

You are responsible for the images you create in your own mind. So, if you spend time and energy imagining the worst case scenarios in your life, then you are physically and emotionally responding to those images and attracting that very same type of negative energy and circumstance into your life. You must choose to visualize positive, inspirational, and uplifting images, in order to create a vibrational match for what you *do* want to attract in your life.

This is the power of visualization.

> **Formulate and stamp indelibly on your mind a mental picture of yourself as succeeding. Hold this picture tenaciously. Never permit it to fade. Your mind will seek to develop the picture.**
> Dr. Norman Vincent Peale

Create your day with this simple visualization.

Sit in a comfortable upright position, close your eyes, and bring your hands together, fingertips touching in your lap, with your spine nice and straight. Now take several slow, deep breaths, inhaling through your nose and exhaling through your mouth. Concentrate on the rise and fall of your stomach and chest with each breath and, with each breath, find yourself becoming more and more relaxed. Now, just let your breathing find its own natural rhythm—slow, steady, and relaxed. Imagine a radiant white light slowly coming up the left side of your body—starting at your left foot and gradually coming up through your left leg, the left side of your torso, shoulders, neck, and face, moving right up to the top of your head, and then slowly moving down the right side of your face, neck, shoulders, torso, hip, and leg, filling each and every cell in your body with radiant white light. Now, go ahead and do this twice more at your own pace, visualizing and experiencing pure white light coming up the left side of your body and down the right side.

With your fingertips still joined in your lap, begin a period of concentration. You may choose to concentrate on a visual symbol or image such as a flower, a source of white light or a still lake—or you may wish to silently repeat a word, seed thought, or a mantra such as "Peace" or "Joy" or "I am love." Silently repeat the image or thought over and over without letting any other thoughts come into your mind. If your mind does begin to wander, just bring it gently back to your point of concentration and know that your ability to stay focused will increase with practice.

Next is receptivity and observation. Separate your hands and place them palms facing upward in your lap, relax your mind, and just notice and observe wherever your tension goes—to thoughts, memories, planning, images, worries, sensations, or insights. Just notice and observe from a neutral position.

And now, completion. Close both of your hands lightly and, again, imagine a luminous white light surrounding you, filling you and protecting you. While you are still surrounded by this white light, visualize this day the way you would like it to go. You may have to adjust to unforeseen circumstances and events that show up, but go ahead and create your day the way you want it to be, paying special attention to how *you* want to be, act, and feel today. Visualize yourself manifesting the qualities you choose for yourself, such as love, joy, courage, strength, patience, and perseverance. See yourself interacting with others with calm, self-assurance, enthusiasm, and clarity. See yourself communicating clearly, stating your desires and intentions, asking for and getting the nurturing you want.

Now, see the specific steps that you will take to achieve your most important goals, and create your day the way you want it to go. See the faces and hear the voices of important people in your life congratulating you on the achievement of your goals and the quality of your being. And now, imagine the emotions you will feel when you are living your day the way you want it to go, and create those feelings in your body right now.

Take a few deep breaths, and once again, place your awareness on the rise and fall of your stomach and your chest as you breathe deeply in and out. Then, when you're ready, slowly open your eyes, and know that this will be a beautiful day.

Aim not for what you are,
but for what you could be.

Lucas Hellmer

Your vision book.

Your vision book is probably your most valuable tool. It is your map of the future, a tangible representation of where you are going. It represents your dreams, your goals, and your ideal life. Because your mind responds strongly to visual stimulation—by representing your desires with pictures and images you will actually strengthen and enhance their vibrational level. The saying "A picture is worth a thousand words" certainly holds true here. Visual images and pictures will stimulate your emotions, and your emotions are the vibrational energy that activates the Law of Attraction.

You have already defined your dreams.
Now, it's time to illustrate them visually.

This world is but a canvas
to our imaginations.

Henry David Thoreau

Create a personal vision book that clearly depicts the future you wish to create. Find pictures that represent or symbolize the experiences, feelings, and possessions you want to attract into your life, and place them in your book. Have fun with the process! Use photographs, magazine cutouts, pictures from the Internet—whatever inspires you. Be creative. Include not only pictures, but anything that speaks to you. Consider including a picture of yourself in your book. If you do, choose one that was taken in a happy moment. You will also want to post your affirmations, inspirational words, quotations, and thoughts here. Choose words and images that inspire you and make you feel good.

This is a book unlike any other.
You are the author, you are the artist.
This is your map.

We have created a unique series of vision books designed specifically for adults, teens and children complete with inspirational words, quotations, affirmations and blank templates for you to create your own. This book is a sacred space—a place to define and honor your dreams, goals, and desires.

Sample of completed Vision Book

Your vision book is a book unlike any other. *You* are the author. . . just add dreams!

To order, please visit our website at **www.dreambigcollection.com**

You can use your vision book to depict goals and dreams in all areas of your life, or in just one specific area that you are focusing on. Keep your life purpose in mind and refer to the list you created when defining your dreams. Keep it neat, and be selective about what you place in your vision book. It's a good idea to avoid creating a cluttered or chaotic book—you don't want to attract chaos into your life. Remember, these are your *dreams*, so choose them well. Use only the words and images that *best* represent your purpose, your ideal future, and that inspire positive emotions in you. There is beauty in simplicity and in clarity. Too many images and too much information will be distracting and harder to focus on.

If you are working on visualizing and creating changes in many areas of your life, then you may want to use more than one vision book. For instance, you might use one vision book for your personal goals and dreams and another for career and financial goals. You might even want to keep your career vision book at the office or on your desk as a means of inspiration and affirmation.

How to use your vision book.

Try keeping your vision book on the nightstand next to your bed. Leave it standing in an open position as often as you are comfortable with, and spend time each morning and evening visualizing, affirming, believing, and internalizing your goals. The time you spend visualizing in the evening just before bed is especially powerful. The thoughts and images that are present in your mind during the last forty-five minutes before going to sleep are the ones that will replay themselves repeatedly in your subconscious mind through-out the night, and the thoughts and images that you begin each day with will help you to create a vibrational match for the future you desire.

As some time goes by, and your dreams begin to manifest, look at those images that represent your achievements, and feel gratitude for how well the Law of Attraction is working in your life. Acknowledge that it is working. Don't remove the pictures or images that represent the goals you've already achieved. These are powerful visual reminders of what you have already consciously and deliberately attracted into your life.

Remember to write down the date you created your vision book. The universe loves speed, and you will be amazed at just how quickly the Law of Attraction responds to your energy, commitment, and desires. Much like a time capsule, this book will document your personal journey, your dreams, and your achievements for that particular year. It will become a record of your growth, awareness, and expansion that you will want to keep and reflect back upon in years to come.

*The biggest adventure you can ever take
is to live the life of your dreams.*
Oprah Winfrey

It's a good idea to create a new vision book each year. As you continue to grow, evolve, and expand, your dreams and aspirations will also continue to grow, evolve, and expand. This will help you continue to stay focused, motivated, and inspired. You might want to make this a new tradition within your family. If you have children, or younger siblings, help them to create their own book, and encourage their dreams too. You will be amazed at how truly insightful, empowering, inspirational, and fun this process can be.

These vision books are meant to be kept and cherished. They chronicle not only your dreams, but your growth and achievements. There is nothing more precious than your dreams, and this book is the face of your dreams. These beautiful words and pictures represent *your* future. They create a vibrational match for what you want to attract and create in your life.

Using your vision book:

- ❖ Look at your vision book often and feel the inspiration it provides.
- ❖ Hold it in your hands and really internalize the future it represents.
- ❖ Read your affirmations and inspirational words aloud.
- ❖ See yourself living in that manner.
- ❖ Feel yourself in the future you have designed.
- ❖ Believe it is already yours.
- ❖ Be grateful for the good that is already present in your life.
- ❖ Acknowledge any goals you have already achieved.
- ❖ Acknowledge the changes you have seen and felt.
- ❖ Acknowledge the presence of God in your life.
- ❖ Acknowledge the Law of Attraction at work in your life.
- ❖ Look at it just before going to bed and first thing upon rising.

Envision your future.
Imagine the possibilities.
Know they are real.

A dream is your creative vision for your life in the future. You must break out of your current comfort zone and become comfortable with the unfamiliar and the unknown.

Denis Waitley

(12)
ATTITUDE

Your attitude can make or break almost any situation.

It is the energy you bring into the room. You can have a positive attitude about the events in your life, or you can come from a place of complaint and misery. *You decide.* You can consciously choose to respond in a positive way to almost *any* event or circumstance—a positive attitude is simply a choice you make.

You can change your attitude and change your life.

> *Any fact facing us is not as important*
> *as our attitude toward it, for that*
> *determines our success or failure.*
>
> Dr. Norman Vincent Peale

Now, we all know people with negative attitudes. They are the ones who constantly complain, whine, and moan. Nothing seems to go right for them. They are the perpetual victims in life. They're unpleasant to be around, and they seem to quite literally "bring us down." This is because they are operating at a *lower* frequency, and through the Law of Attraction they are attracting even more to complain about. The reason they tend to stay "stuck" in their negative lifestyles is because they are constantly focusing their thoughts and energy on their negative present and negative past. By doing so, they are creating the same future over and over. Remember, what you continually talk about comes about.

On the other hand, we also know people with positive attitudes—the ones who always seem to be happy, the ones who really seem to have a handle on things in their life. They are more fun, their energy feels great to be around, and they are operating at a *higher* frequency. Good things always seem to "just come their way." No wonder they are happy! Through the Law of Attraction, they are actively participating in the creation of a happy life by focusing on and appreciating the positive aspects of their current life, and they have positive expectations for a great future life.

> *People are just as happy*
> *as they make up their minds to be.*
>
> Abraham Lincoln

Surround yourself with these positive, nourishing, uplifting people whenever you can. Spend your time with spiritually evolved people who love and support you in healthy ways—those who encourage your growth and applaud your successes. Wrap yourself in a support network of inspirational people with positive attitudes and energy.

You may also want to consider finding a place of worship, charity organization, or some other group that is in alignment with your desires for personal growth. You can also form your own small group of people who share common interests and goals. There is power in numbers, and a higher mindset becomes present with a group such as this. By gathering together on a regular basis with a stated purpose and intention you will all experience greater growth and results in a shorter period of time. The assembly of a mastermind group like this provides a unique forum for shared ideas, feedback, brain-storming, honesty, accountability, and inspiration. It has been a proven tool for growth and success on a business level for many years. Henry Ford, Thomas Edison, Napoleon Hill, Harvey Firestone, and Andrew Carnegie were all members of similar mastermind groups.

> *I never did a day's work in my life.*
> *It was all fun.*
>
> Thomas Edison

So, how do we deal with the negative people in our lives? First of all, remember that you are not responsible for their level of growth or consciousness. You can only be an example to them and keep your energy vibration as high as possible. You cannot teach them anything they are not ready or willing to learn. Keep in mind, however, that nobody is completely negative. You can focus on the good qualities that do exist in them and appreciate the qualities they have that *are* working within the context of your relationship. You can also acknowledge the things about them that you *do* like or admire, and this may encourage them to express more of those positive qualities.

Don't judge the negative people in your life—simply limit your time and interaction with them as much as possible (avoid them completely if you can) and try to be an example of a more positive attitude. Obviously, if these people are family members or coworkers it is difficult to avoid them altogether, but do your best to avoid any issues of conflict, keep your attitude positive, and don't engage yourself emotionally in conflict when it does arise. Ultimately, you will need to decide whether or not you want to keep these relationships in your life at all.

Your attitude is crucial—it affects your emotions, and your emotions, in turn, affect the energy field around you and simultaneously place your order with the universe for more of the same. Take a close, honest look at your attitude in the various areas of your life. Is there room for improvement?

> *The art of being happy lies in the*
> *power of extracting happiness*
> *from common things.*
>
> Henry Ward Beecher

Try changing your attitude and finding pleasure in the simple things in life. We all have daily tasks and mundane chores that we have typically dreaded in the past. Why not challenge yourself to turn even those into opportunities for growth? Change your approach to taking out the garbage and paying the bills. These are necessary routines and they're not going to go away, so you might as well try to enjoy them! Put some music on as you clean the kitchen and empty the trash. Learn to bless each bill you pay, and send it off with love. Be grateful for how fortunate you really are and for how many luxuries you have in your life. You can completely shift your energy, have a little fun, and look at these things as opportunities to care for yourself and make a contribution to the people you love, rather than as burdensome chores. When you can learn to approach every single task and situation with an attitude of joy and enthusiasm, you will notice an immediate difference in your life. Life is *literally* what you make of it.

Remember, this life is a journey, and it's meant to be enjoyed. Choose to maintain a positive attitude. Be happy. Be grateful. Be loving and generous. Surround yourself with positive people and energy. Look forward to each new day with the excitement and the wonder of a small child. Who knows what amazing things will happen next! Have faith, and have *fun*. Your future will unfold in miraculous ways.

Most people are searching for happiness.
They're looking for it. They're trying to find it
in someone or something outside of themselves.
That's a fundamental mistake.
Happiness is something that you are,
and it comes from the way you think.

Wayne Dyer

Gratitude and Appreciation.

The best attitude you can possibly aspire to is one of *gratitude and appreciation*. Being truly grateful for what is already present in your life will automatically and effortlessly attract more good into your life. Make a conscious decision to appreciate and acknowledge all that you have already been blessed with. These emotions are of the highest vibrational frequency, and through the Law of Attraction they will attract even more to be thankful for.

Try to be grateful for even the difficult and challenging situations that arise in your life. It is often through these situations that we experience the most profound spiritual and emotional growth. You can learn to view each apparent obstacle as an opportunity to develop a new quality, strength, skill, insight, or wisdom and be grateful for the lessons. Each and every challenge is another opportunity for growth and expansion.

Rise to these occasions, and appreciate all that you are learning in the process. Keeping your attitude positive and appreciative through these times will not only help to avoid attracting more of these difficult situations into your life—it will also create a field of positive energy that will attract more of what you *do* want.

Happiness is itself a kind of gratitude.

Joseph Wood Krutch

Of all the attitudes we can acquire, surely
the attitude of gratitude is the most important,
and by far the most life-changing.

Zig Ziglar

A Token of Gratitude.

Try carrying a small token, stone, crystal, or some other meaningful object with you each day in your pocket. Throughout the day, each time you reach into your pocket for your money or keys it will serve as a tangible reminder to stop and think of something you have to be grateful for. This is a great way to increase your awareness of all that you have to be appreciative of. Take a moment to breathe, and really feel the emotion of gratitude. This simple mindfulness technique helps to raise your vibrational frequency and keep you in a state of constant gratitude.

Joy is an attitude;
it is the presence of love—
for self and others. It comes from a feeling
of inner peace, the ability to give and receive,
and appreciation of the self and others.
It is a state of gratitude and compassion,
a feeling of connection to
your higher self.

Unknown

Your Gratitude Journal.

Start keeping a daily gratitude and acknowledgement journal. This is a necessary and valuable tool in the development of your growth and awareness. Each daily entry is not intended to be a long, drawn out "diary" sort of thing, just a short, simple list of five things that you are grateful for on that particular day. This is a place to honor and appreciate the good in your life on a daily basis.

Gratitude. Each evening, before going to bed, take a few minutes to review your day. Think about the day's events. Become aware of how many good things actually happened on that day, and remember to appreciate even the challenges that you encountered. Select the five things, people, or events that you are most grateful for. There is no right or wrong here, just whatever or whoever you are sincerely grateful for on that particular day. It may be the warm sun on your face, a cool breeze, a kind word, a friend, or just feeling good about what you got accomplished that day. It may be the way you handled a particular situation that would have thrown you into a tailspin in the past. *Anything* you are grateful for. As you write them in your journal, *feel* the gratitude and appreciation. Give thanks.

Acknowledgement. Take a moment to acknowledge the changes that are occurring for you personally. Write them down. Acknowledge just how well the Law of Attraction is working in your life. Write down any specific event where the Law of Attraction was at work—the parking space you envisioned, the meeting you wanted to schedule, the bonus check you received, the grade you wanted, the person who said yes when you asked them out. Miracles can and do occur on a daily basis. They are happening all around you. Honor them, and notice them. Through acknowledgement, you will become more and more aware of the amazing synchronicity that is already at work in your life.

Make the time you spend in contemplation and writing in your gratitude and acknowledgement journal a sacred part of your daily routine. Your continued expressions of joy and gratitude will draw even greater joy, love, and abundance into your life.

You will begin to notice a change in your perception of each day's events. You will become more aware of the positive things that happen all around you every single day. Your focus will shift, your energy will shift, and you will begin to appreciate how blessed you already are. And . . . the Law of Attraction will respond to the higher vibration you are creating.

Enjoy the journey.
Live each day in joy and gratitude.
Acknowledge the presence of God in your life.

> *There is a calmness to a life*
> *lived in gratitude, a quiet joy.*
>
> Ralph H. Blum

In our desire to make this easier for you we have created a beautiful Gratitude journal that you can utilize for this purpose. It contains dated pages for daily entries of what you are grateful for and weekly inspirational quotes. It also has blank pages where you can record any personal acknowledgements of how the Law of Attraction is working in your life. You can order a copy from **www.dreambigcollection.com.**

(13)
PRAYER AND MEDITATION

**Prayer and meditation are our
connections to God, to our higher power.**

Take time each day to step away from the clutter and the noise. A daily commitment to spend time in this still, quiet place is a commitment to clarity and inner peace. We need this time and space in our lives in order to remember who we really are, what's important, and where our personal truth lies. It is our time to calm the spirit and soothe the soul. It restores balance in our lives, and it reconnects us to our Source.

It is through prayer, meditation, and contemplation that we are best able to hear our own inner voice. This is a time to pause and connect not only with God, but with ourselves and our creative subconscious mind. This time spent within nourishes us on the deepest levels physically, emotionally, and spiritually.

Some people say that through prayer we are talking to God, and through meditation we are listening to him. Through quiet contemplation we can look inside and reconnect with our own deeper truth and wisdom. Through each of these practices, we are opening our hearts and our minds and preparing ourselves to receive divine guidance and inspiration.

> *The value of consistent prayer is not that
> He will hear us; but that we will hear Him.*
>
> *William McGill*

If you have never meditated before, here's a simple structure you can use to begin.

Find a quiet and comfortable place, and set aside at least ten to fifteen minutes of undisturbed time. Sit comfortably with your back straight, but not stiff. Take a deep breath, relax, and do your best to put aside all thoughts of the past and the future, keeping your focus right here in the present moment.

Become aware of your breathing by focusing your attention on the sensation of the air that is moving in and out of your body as you breathe. Feel your stomach gently rising and falling as you breathe in . . . and breathe out. Feel the coolness and warmth of the air that enters and leaves your nostrils as you inhale and exhale. Notice the way each breath changes and is different.

Observe your thoughts as they come and go. When thoughts come up in your mind, don't ignore them or suppress them—simply notice them and let them drift on by, always returning your focus back to your breathing.

If you find yourself getting carried away by your thoughts, just observe where your mind went, and without judging, simply return to your breathing once again. Let your breath serve as an anchor for your thoughts.

As the time comes to a close, sit quietly, and slowly return your thoughts and consciousness to your surroundings. Get up gradually and stretch for a moment or two. You are now ready to go back to your normal routine relaxed and refreshed.

If we know the divine art of concentration,
if we know the divine art of meditation,
if we know the divine art of contemplation,
easily and consciously we can unite
the inner world and the outer world.

Sri Chinmoy

There are many ways to meditate, but in general they consist of simply being still and quiet for a period of time and focusing your attention on either your breath or a mantra of some sort. If you are new to the practice of meditation—your thoughts will drift, and your mind will wander at first. Remember not to be hard on yourself when this happens. This is just part of learning how to meditate. I love the metaphor that it's like standing on the side of a river watching boats drift by. Every once in awhile you will discover that you have gotten into one of the boats and are floating down the river. Just simply get out of the boat, climb back onto the river bank and start observing the boats (your thoughts) again. Don't worry about whether or not you're getting it "right." Your ability to stay focused will increase with time and practice.

The regular practice of meditation will help clear your mind of distractions, cleanse your thoughts, and enhance your spiritual connection. It renews the spirit, relaxes the body, and calms the soul. Meditation is a tool for reflection and inquiring within, and it is one of the best ways to still your thoughts in order to receive divine guidance. Through the practice of meditation you will begin to become even more aware of your subtle intuitive impulses, insights, ideas, emotions, and inspirations.

Meditation is the dissolution
of thoughts in eternal awareness or
pure consciousness without objectification,
knowing without thinking, merging
finitude in infinity.

Voltaire

Spend time each day in quiet contemplation, prayer, or meditation.

Here is a simple invocation you can use to begin.

In seeking to transform our lives,

We ask for guidance and clarity.

We ask that we find our purpose, our mission in life.

We ask for divine inspiration.

We ask to be of service.

We ask for help in releasing any old negative or limiting thought patterns.

We ask that our thoughts and actions unfold for the greater good of all people.

We ask that miracles unfold not only in our own lives, but in the lives of others.

We are thankful.

We ask for peace.

We ask for harmony.

We ask to make a difference in the world.

There is an inner alchemy that takes place through prayer and meditation. They help you to empty your mind of worries and negative thoughts, and they make room for it to be filled with joy, bliss, and love. These are *transformational* processes that will change you on a cellular level. They will literally change your brain wave patterns, increasing your good feelings and creating a sense of happiness. In addition to that, the vibrational frequency of these positive emotions is in perfect harmony with what you want to attract into your life.

Through prayer, contemplation, and meditation you are aligning yourself with a higher power and opening yourself up to the unlimited potential and infinite wisdom of the universe. Your devotion and commitment to spiritual growth and expansion will serve to alter your consciousness and open you up to a greater awareness of the miracles, circumstances, possibilities, and synchronicity already at work in your life. Through prayer you are also *acknowledging* God. You are *acknowledging* that there is a higher power at work in your life.

Prayer, contemplation, and meditation are essential, powerful tools in your life.
Make a commitment to use them.
They are the way in.

If you believe, you will receive
whatever you ask for in prayer.
Mathew 21:22

(14)

ACTION

Take action.

Start by opening your mind and your heart. Commit yourself to the daily use of the tools that we have provided you with, and strive to become more aware of the amazing synchronicity that already exists in your life. Sweep away any lingering negative thoughts or emotions. Sweep away any doubt. And then take actions each and every day that will move you toward your purpose and the fulfillment of your dreams.

There are two kinds of action you can take.

Obvious Action
We are all familiar with obvious action. Some examples of obvious action are: if you want a new car, going out to test drive all of the cars you are interested in, choosing the exact make and model you want, and saving 10 percent of your income in a "car account." If you want to become a doctor, then obvious actions would be things like applying to medical school, taking courses in premed, and so on. Obvious actions are logical, somewhat predictable action steps that stem from the conscious mind.

Inspired action
Inspired action is much less linear, and oftentimes will seem to be completely unrelated to your ultimate goals. Once you begin to get in touch with your higher consciousness by using

your vision book, affirmations, visualization, daily gratitude journal, meditations, and prayer, the universe will start responding by sending you the ideas, people, opportunities, money, and other resources you need to fulfill your desires and make your dreams a reality.

You are going to find that you have inspired ideas, intuitive impulses, and gentle proddings from your dreams. You must act on them. Let your curiosity and interests guide you. This is *inspired action*. It is action born of your willingness to trust your intuition, follow your hunches, and listen to your inner voice. Inspired action is a real demonstration of your belief and positive expectation. This type of action is funneled through the subconscious mind, and it is inspired by your awareness and openness to the possibilities all around you. It speaks of your trust and of your connection. It takes faith to move forward with inspired action because it is far less familiar to us than obvious action.

Dreams pass into the reality of action.
From the actions stems the dream again;
and this interdependence produces
the highest form of living.

Anais Nin

Often your intuitive nudges will be very subtle, and they may seem to have no direct relationship to the fulfillment of your dreams, but if you follow them, your life will become very magical. Based on your desires, you will soon be led down a wonderful path of transformation, growth and fulfillment. This path may look quite different from the one you originally imagined. Learn to trust your deeper self. Learn to trust the process. Learn to trust God and the universe. You are cocreating with a higher power that knows more and sees more than you ever can.

So, be prepared to take not only the obvious logical steps, which would lead you in the direction of your dreams and aspirations, but take the less obvious ones as well. Have faith and be willing to move forward with the confidence and conviction of your desires, knowing that the universe will support you in your efforts. Taking *any* action is simply a logical extension of your belief and your trust. If you didn't really *believe* something was possible you wouldn't take any action at all.

The basic difference here is that *obvious action* is pretty much just up to you, and you alone, whereas *inspired action* is you, using the power of your subconscious mind, believing and cocreating with God and the universe. A combination of these two is ideal. Give it to God, *and* be willing to do the work!

> *Thought is the blossom;*
> *language the bud;*
> *action the fruit behind it.*
> Ralph Waldo Emerson

Remember, through the Law of Attraction, the universe will provide you with all that you need in order to reach your goals. You will attract the necessary resources, ideas, and people into your life. It's up to *you* to recognize them, though, and it's up to *you* to follow through on these inspired thoughts and ideas.

Everything you want is out there waiting for you to ask. Everything you want also wants you, but you have to take action to get it.

The universe wants you to succeed.

Expect your every need to be met.
Expect the answer to every problem.
Expect abundance on every level.

Eileen Caddy

Start making room in your life for the beauty and abundance that is rightfully yours. Remember how powerful you are. It is not enough to dream and desire; you must actually be willing to take action both internally and externally toward creating the life of your dreams. You must also be disciplined enough to follow through with the daily rituals that will keep you in a state of positive vibration that is a match for the future you desire.

So, make a commitment to take these actions each day. Integrate these rituals into your daily routine:

Daily Rituals

1. Begin each day by spending at least five minutes focusing your mind on your desires, goals, and intentions. Get comfortable, close your eyes, and visualize all of your goals and desires as already being fulfilled. Really feel the emotions of that reality. See your day going exactly as you would like it to.

2. Use your tools each day. Your vision book, gratitude journal, gratitude token, and affirmations will all provide tangible external inspiration and positively shift your energetic field. Make a commitment to really use these tools daily, and apply them in your life.

3. Start paying attention to how often you have emotional responses each day that are not in alignment with your purpose or creating the life you desire. Whenever you become aware of this, make the shift. Change your thoughts and feelings to those that are a vibrational match for what you want to attract. Stay focused on the things that bring you joy, and keep your expectations positive.

4. Remember the importance of gratitude and appreciation in all areas of your life. Make time in each day to connect with God and with yourself.

5. Take *action* every day that is in alignment with your purpose, goals, and desires. Be mindful and aware. Act upon your inspired ideas. Trust your emotions and intuition. Pay attention and respond to the feedback you are getting. Make daily steps in the direction of your dreams.

6. Acknowledge that the Law of Attraction is working in your life. With every evidence of its effect, acknowledge and give thanks. The more you acknowledge that it is working, the more it will work. It's that simple.

See where your own energy wants to go,
not where you think it should go.
Do something because it feels right,
not because it makes sense.
Follow the spiritual impulse.

Mary Hayes-Grieco

Hold tight to the purpose and vision you have created for your future and own them with every ounce of your being. Keep all of your actions in alignment with your higher purpose, and keep your intentions pure. You will attract amazing and beautiful things into your life. So, be fearless, have fun, and be willing to take a few risks. Reach for the stars, and know that you are supported in every way.

Move forward with confidence in the direction of your dreams and desires. Believe that they are not only possible, but that they are already in progress.

If you have the courage to begin,
you have the courage
to succeed.

David Viscott

(15)
BELIEVE

Believe.

The tools we have provided will prepare the soil, but *you* must plant the seeds and create an environment that will nourish their growth and expansion. Now that you have placed your order with the universe, you must have faith. Be resilient. Trust that it is already so, and give it to God. Although you may not know the exact path to your dreams, the way *will* reveal itself. Be willing to take action. Once you commit to your dreams, the Law of Attraction will take care of the rest. Life will present you with the people, circumstances, and whatever else is needed to bring them into reality.

> *You must be the change*
> *you want to see in the world.*
> Mahatma Gandhi

We hope that you will make a personal commitment to creating a better life for yourself and a better world for all of us. Imagine the possibilities. Envision just how amazing this world will become as we all make the shift into awareness, into a positive state of being. We can shift the energy of the entire planet, one person at a time. Through our awareness, generosity, commitment, and intention we can truly begin to live in accordance with the natural laws of the universe and restore our balance with nature. We can create a world filled with love, joy, harmony, and peace.

> *Give up your small ambitions,*
> *come and save the world.*
>
> St. Frances Xavier Cabrini

We have been living for far too long in a state of oblivion, completely unaware of just how powerful we really are. Now is the time to reclaim our power. Now is the time to be fully accountable for the state of our lives and the state of the world we live in. Now is the time to reclaim the joy and abundance that are rightfully ours.

The Law of Attraction is always in motion.
You have already begun.
The future is yours.

See it. Feel it. Believe it.

> *Just take the first step in faith.*
> *You don't have to see the whole staircase.*
> *Just take the first step.*
>
> Martin Luther King Jr.

To fully live the Law of Attraction and create the life of your dreams:

- ❖ Use your affirmations daily.
- ❖ Use your gratitude journal daily.
- ❖ Use your vision book daily.
- ❖ Spend time each day in prayer or meditation.
- ❖ Stay true to your purpose.
- ❖ Believe in your dreams.
- ❖ Focus on the positive.
- ❖ Live in a state of constant gratitude.
- ❖ Visualize the life you desire.
- ❖ Be passionate about life.
- ❖ Be generous.
- ❖ Be happy.
- ❖ Do the things that make you feel good.
- ❖ Find the best in every situation.
- ❖ Listen to your inner voice.
- ❖ Respond to internal and external feedback.
- ❖ Follow through on your inspired thoughts.
- ❖ Be aware of the miracles all around you.
- ❖ Be willing to take risks.
- ❖ Move forward with confidence.
- ❖ Acknowledge the changes you see and feel.
- ❖ Remember the Law of Attraction.
- ❖ Trust.
- ❖ Release it to God, Source, the universe.

This is the key to unlocking the Law of Attraction. This is the key to your future.

**If you have questions, comments, or if you
would like more information about
Living the Law of Attraction, please visit
www.askjackcanfield.com**

Please refer to our website
for additional products and
information.
www.dreambigcollection.com

ABOUT THE AUTHORS

Jack Canfield is the cocreator and coauthor of the *New York Times* #1 best-selling book series *Chicken Soup for the Soul,* which currently has 146 titles and over 100 million copies in print in 47 languages. His publications also include *The Success Principles: How to Get from Where You Are to Where You Want to Be, The Power of Focus,* and *The Aladdin Factor.*

Jack is also known as one of the teachers featured in the hit movie and the best-selling book *The Secret.* He has appeared on over one thousand radio and television shows including *Oprah, Montel, Larry King Live,* the *Today Show, 20/20* and his own PBS special: *The Secret to Living the Law of Attraction.*

He is also the founder and CEO of the *Self Esteem Seminars, Inc.* and *The Canfield Group,* which trains entrepreneurs, corporate leaders, managers, and sales professionals and educators in how to accelerate the achievement of their personal, professional, and financial goals. Jack has been presenting these universal principles and breakthrough strategies for more than thirty-five years to corporations, government agencies, and universities in over thirty countries.

Jack and his wife, Inga, along with their three children—Christopher, Riley, and Travis—reside in Santa Barbara, California. For more information on Jack, go to www.jackcanfield.com.

D.D. Watkins has always believed that all things are possible. She is a working mom, successful entrepreneur, and artist who admittedly thrives on challenge, inspiration, and personal growth.

Over the years she has designed and created art installations throughout the world. Her most recent commissions have included architectural, interior, and graphic design projects. As a lover of words, wisdom, books, and beauty, she is currently exploring the fields of writing and plein air painting. She has chosen to make her home in Santa Barbara, California.